# MARIAN REFLECTIONS

Xmas 2001
Theresa Marozza

# MARIAN REFLECTIONS

## The Angelus Messages of Pope John Paul II

Edited and Annotated
by
Rev. David O. Brown, O.S.M.

AMI Press, Inc.
Washington, N.J. 07882

Imprimatur: Rev. Msgr. John B. Szymanski
Vicar General
Diocese of Metuchen

N.B. The imprimatur implies nothing more than that the material contained in this publication has been examined by diocean censors and that nothing contrary to faith and morals has been found therein.

Cover photo.

The Annunciation is depicted in this detail of a painting by an unknown Tuscan artist near the end of the thirteenth century. It is in the Servite Church of the SS. Annunziata in Florence, Italy and has long been the object of very special devotion.



Library of Congress Catalogue Card No: 90-82367

ISBN 0-911988-96-3

To all my sisters and brothers

# Contents

## The Angelus

The Angel of the Lord declared unto Mary.

And she conceived by the Holy Spirit.

Hail Mary, etc.

Behold the handmaid of the Lord

Be it done unto me according to thy Word.

Hail Mary, etc.

And the Word was made flesh.

And dwelt among us.

Hail Mary, etc.

V. Pray for us, O Holy Mother of God.

R. That we may be made worthy of the promises of Christ.

Let us pray.

Pour forth we beseech Thee, O Lord, thy grace into our hearts, that we, to whom the Incarnation of Christ thy Son was made known by the message of an angel, may by his Passion and Cross, be brought to the glory of his Resurrection. Through the same Christ Our Lord.

Amen.

## Regina Coeli

*This antiphon to the Blessed Virgin (literally Queen of Heaven) dates to the twelfth century. It is said in place of the Angelus during the fifty days of Easter.*

Queen of heaven, rejoice, alleluia.

For He Whom thou did deserve to bear, alleluia,

Has risen as He said, alleluia.

Pray for us to God, alleluia.

V. Rejoice and be glad, O Virgin Mary, alleluia.
R. Because the Lord has truly risen, alleluia.

Let us pray

O God, Who by the resurrection of thy Son,
Our Lord Jesus Christ,
has been pleased to fill the world with joy,
grant, we beseech Thee,
that through the intercession of the Virgin Mary,
his Mother,
we may receive the joys of eternal life,
through the same Christ Our Lord.

Amen.

# Introduction

Nearly every Sunday at noon, Pope John Paul II recites the Angelus with the Christian faithful who gather in St. Peter's Square to receive his blessing. He usually delivers a short spiritual reflection before the recitation of the Angelus. From Easter 1983 to Easter 1984 his messages were generally theological reflections on the place of Mary in the scheme of salvation. Two themes predominate. While she was the Mother of the Lord, Mary was also a believer, a model and type for all believers. She is likewise Mother of the Church and so a model and type for the Church.

As we listen, reflect and pray with the Holy Father, we may expect to see our appreciation, our love and devotion to Mary grow and deepen.

There are forty-eight messages in this series. Some Sundays when the Pope was away from Rome, there were no messages. At other times some special event, such as a canonization, took precedence.

The notes following the Angelus are my attempt to simplify the complex thoughts which the Holy Father had compressed into his very short messages. Only occasionally are there any real additions to his thought.

Rev. David O. Brown O.S.M.

*April 10, 1983*

# Mary's Easter

## "Regina Caeli, laetare, alleluia!"

The ancient and beautiful antiphon that we will soon recite, completely interspersed with the "alleluia" of exultation, speaks to us very well of the joy of the Lord's mother over the resurrection of her divine Son and, with her and in her, the joy of the Church and of all of us.

The Gospels do not speak to us of any apparition of the Risen Jesus to his mother: this ineffable mystery of joy remains under the veil of a mystical silence. It is certain, however, that she, the first to be redeemed, just as she was in a special way near her Son's cross (Jn 19:25), also had a privileged experience of the Risen Christ, such as to cause in her a most intense joy, unique among that of all the other creatures who were saved by the blood of Christ.

Mary is a guide for us in the knowledge of the mysteries of the Lord: and just as in her and with her we understand the meaning of the cross, so in her and with her we are able to understand the significance of the resurrection, tasting the joy that comes from such an experience.

Mary, in fact, among all creatures, "believed," from the very beginning, all that the Word, becoming flesh in her, did

---

From *L'Osservatore Romano* No. 16 (780) 18 April 1983
Title: "Mary Our Guide in Knowing the Mysteries of the Lord"

in the world for the salvation of the world. In an ascent of exultation based on faith, her joy passed from that of the "Magnificat," full of hope, to that purest joy, no longer a shadow of decline, over her Son's triumph over sin and death.

Mary is the one who "cooperated," as the Second Vatican Council says, "in an utterly singular way in the Savior's work of restoring supernatural life to souls, by her obedience, faith, hope and burning charity" (*Lumen Gentium,* 61). And now "she cares for the brethren of her Son who still journey on earth surrounded by dangers and difficulties, until they are led to their happy fatherland" (ibid, 62).

Brothers and sisters, may Mary's path be also ours. May her joy be ours. And just as she, joyous over her Son's resurrection, is the source of our joy, "*causa nostrae laetitiae,*" so let us commit ourselves to being Mary's joy, allowing Christ the Redeemer to form in us the supernatural life, right up to the eternal joy of our happy fatherland. "With her, the Queen of Heaven!"

* * *

1. St. John's Gospel tells us that not everything which Jesus said and did is written down (Jn 21:25). Our Holy Father Pope John Paul II refers to one such event hidden from us. It is the meeting of Mary and Jesus who has just been raised from the dead. This event is hidden in mystical silence.

2. These words "mystical silence" are profound. Whenever we consider certain aspects of our faith, we engage the deepest part of ourselves. Hence the word "mystical."

3. In each of the Pope's talks, we will see that while the focus is on one aspect of Mary's life and work—here her joy at the resurrection of Jesus—he will refer as well to some other aspect of her life or a privilege. Here he mentions two: Mary was the first to be redeemed, and she stood near the Cross on which her Son died.

4. As we recall the scene in the Gospel in the home of Zechariah and Elizabeth where Mary prayed the "Magnificat," we remember

it as a time of joy. It was a joy which was built on hope and expectation. Mary's joy at the resurrection was of a deeper "purer" kind. Each, however, was built on faith. Mary believed.

5. Mary is our model because she obeyed, believed, hoped and loved with a burning charity.

6. One of the favorite themes of Pope John Paul II is Mary's loving care for each of us. In this she is the "cause of our joy."

7. Mary is our example, but we in turn must respond. We must follow her example and allow the Redeemer to bring to completion in us the fullness of the redemption.

# Mary, the First Fruit of the Redemption

Again at the festive meeting of this Sunday we direct our thoughts to the Blessed Virgin Mary with that intensity of sentiment inspired by Easter, which we have recently celebrated.

Today wc wish to consider in her, Mary, what could be called the "success" of the Paschal Mystery: its "result," its happy outcome. In fact, the Paschal Mystery, the glorification of life, is in time and space the perpetual source of life and, lived in the footsteps of Christ, always bears the fruits of life. Jesus did not die in vain: his death is like that of the seed thrown on the ground: it is fruitful in results. And its most beautiful and most exalting fruit is the glorious triumph of Mary, his mother. She is the most exquisite fruit of the seed of eternal life that God, in Jesus Christ, has sown in the heart of mankind in need of salvation after Adam's sin.

Mary is the greatest "success" of the Paschal Mystery. She is the woman "resulting" perfectly in the order of nature as well as in the order of grace, because more than any other human creature she was able to meditate upon it, understand it, and live it. For the Christian it is impossible to taste the meaning of Easter precinding from how Mary, victorious

---

From *L'Osserevatore Romano* No. 17 (781) 25 April 1983
Title: "Mary Is the Greatest 'Success' of the Paschal Mystery"

over the ancient adversary with Christ and through Christ, experienced it. In the mystery of her heavenly assumption in body and soul the whole Church will celebrate the complete fulfillment of the Paschal Mystery, because in the Mother of God thus glorified, she sees the ideal type and destination of her journey through the course of the centuries.

It is therefore in Mary and with Mary that we can penetrate the meaning of the Paschal Mystery, allowing it to bear in us the immense richness of its effects and its fruits of eternal life. In her and with her, who did not pass from sin to grace, as we all did, but who through a singular privilege, in view of the merits of Christ, was preserved from sin, journeying toward the eternal Easter from the very first moment of her existence. Even more than that, her whole life was an "Easter": a passage, a journey in joy: from the joy of hope at the time of trial to the joy of possession after the triumph over death. Her human person, as we know by solemn definition, in the footsteps of the Risen One, completed in body and soul the Easter passage from death to a glorious eternal life.

After the example of Mary, we too have been called to welcome Christ, who forgives us, redeems us, saves us and carries out in us the Easter passage from death to life.

* * *

1. How do we measure "success"? Pope John Paul teaches us that real success is the success of Jesus in his triumph over sin and death at Easter. It is the success of a seed which is planted and then grows to bud forth with new life.

2. On the first Sunday after Easter the Pope reminds us that Mary is such a "success," and we see in her success the promise given to Adam, fulfilled in Christ and implanted in our hearts as well.

3. Mary more than any other creature was able to penetrate, understand and live the Paschal Mystery. She experienced the struggle and so the victory in Christ. We too are lead into this mystery in Christ and with Mary.

4. When the Holy Father uses the word "type," he wants to teach us that what we see in Mary is the model of what we must see in ourselves. Thus, in the Assumption of Mary, the Church is able to see its own destiny, a resurrection in Christ.

5. The Holy Father uses a play on words which we may miss in English. Speaking in Italian, he uses the word for Easter "Pasqua" which alludes to the Angel in the Book of Exodus who "passes over" the homes of the Hebrews in Egypt. It also refers to their "passage," their journey over the Red Sea. Mary's journey was very special, of course, but it was a passage which began at the first moment of her conception and moved to an eternal Easter.

6. Her life was a passage from joy to joy; from the joy of hope to the joy of possession, from the joy of expectation to the joy of triumph over death.

7. With Mary, we too are called to welcome Christ who forgives us, saves us and brings us from death to eternal life.

*April 24, 1983*

# Death Has No Hold on Mary

There is no happier or more important announcement of our salvation than the one proclaimed by the apostles: "The Lord is truly risen" (Lk 24:34). In Jesus the terrible duel between death and life ends in favor of life. He is the Living One, the Conqueror of the forces of evil, the Lord of history (cf. 2 Cor 135:4; Rev 5:5; 1:8; Phil 2:11). He did not return to the life he had had before—still destined for death—as Lazarus did, but he assumed a new and everlasting life; "Christ, once raised from the dead, will never die again; death has no more power over him" (Rom 6:9).

Jesus draws all the faithful after him, since he is "the first fruits" and "the first-born of the dead" (1 Cor 15:20; Col 1:18). And above all, he draws after him his Mother, glorified in the wake of the Risen One, as the Church has always perceived in harmony with the Virgin's mission in the plan of salvation.

For this reason we too, with Christian generations that have gone before us, have the joy of proclaiming the happy announcement: "Mary is living with the Lord, she is living a full and imperishable life! On her, too, through the grace of Christ, death no longer has any hold!"

This conviction is presupposed in the confident prayer

---

From *L'Osservatore Romano* No. 18 (782) 2 May 1983
Title: "Because of Christ's Grace, Death Has No Hold on Mary"

that at least since the third century the faithful have addressed to Mary, invoking her in the antiphon, *Sub tuum praesidium,* as the holy Mother of God, graced with power, purity and mercy.

With immense joy we contemplate Mary, living and glorified in the wake of the Risen One. In her we see the destiny of the Church prefigured. If we are faithful to Christ, we too will enjoy Mary's destiny and will see the gates of life open before us. May her example confirm our certainty and may her prayer sustain our path and our hope.

Today we are observing the World Day of Prayer for Vocations.

On this Sunday when the liturgy presents for our consideration the figure of the Good Shepherd, we are all called to reflect upon the Church's need for numerous and holy vocations. I would like to exhort you above all to thank the Lord for the increase in vocations which has been noted this past year in not a few dioceses in the world. This renewal is a great comfort.

Although vocations are a gift from God, we must intensify our prayers to invoke from the Lord a sufficient number of workers for his harvest which is currently so abundant.

In this Holy Year, in which we are reliving with special intensity the mystery of the Redemption, may there not be lacking in every parish and in every Christian family special prayers that many may have the joy and the courage to respond to the Lord's call.

I then address my thoughts especially to families, who have such an important role in fostering the development of the seeds of vocation. I hope they will always esteem and appreciate more the gift of a religious vocation from their sons and daughters, feeling honored if the Lord will deem to call one of them to follow him closely in giving himself or herself to God in the priesthood or the religious life.

For this intention, let us now recite the Regina Caeli.

* * *

1. The struggle between good and evil, between life and death is a fact of the human condition. We have experienced it in ourselves. When the Apostles announced that "the Lord is truly risen," it was as if they were predicting final victory while the battle was still raging. This is just what they did. Christ is indeed the Lord of history.

2. The Holy Father makes a very important clarification about the resurrection of Jesus. Jesus rose to a new and everlasting life! It was not the same as when he had called Lazarus from the tomb (Jn 11:44). That was properly call a "resuscitation." Lazarus was to die again later. Jesus lives forever.

3. What the Father had accomplished in Jesus is offered as a promise to each of us. The first to participate in this promise was Mary, the Mother of Jesus. Death no longer has any power over Jesus and now, death has no power over Mary.

4. The hymn *Sub tuum praesidium* dates from the third century.

> "We fly to your protection,
> O Holy Mother of God.
> Do not despise us in our needs.
> Free us, O blessed and glorious virgin
> from every danger."

5. We are happy for the special graces and glory which have been given to Mary by her Son. Still there is more to it than that. We are able to rejoice that the glory she now enjoys is what all the Church is to share. We too are to enter the gates of life if we, like Mary, are faithful to Christ.

6. The Holy Father inserts a special call for vocations in this Angelus message.

*May 22, 1983*
*At Milan*

# Annunciation and Pentecost

## "The Spirit of the Lord Has Filled the Universe, Alleluia!" (Wis 1:7).

This joyful song rises today from the hearts of all the redeemed in the Jubilee Year of the Redemption. The Spirit of God has poured new life into our souls and has given new impetus to the history of salvation: "and so, in the fullness of Easter joy, mankind exults in all the world" (Easter Preface I).

Mary is the sublime testimony of what the Spirit of God can do in man when he renews him in his innermost being and constitutes him a living stone in a new world. Predisposed by the grace of the Redeemer, she responded with faithful obedience to every request of God, to every movement of the Holy Spirit: as a humble handmaid she gave herself a virgin to the Lord; as a considerate sister she was attentive to the needs of others; as a mother she dedicated herself entirely to the person and the mission of her Redeemer Son, becoming his perfect disciple and associating herself generously with him in the one sacrifice that removes sin and reconciles us with the Father. The Holy Spirit gradually lighted up for her the dark pathway of faith, he il-

---

From *L'Osservatore Romano* No. 21 (786) 16 May 1983
Title: "The Annunciation and Pentecost"

luminated every word and action of her Son, he supported her in the pain of Calvary and in the supreme offering. Then, after the Cross, he fashioned her to her Son in glory.

Pentecost therefore speaks to us of Mary's presence in the Church: a praying presence in the Church of the Apostles and in the Church of every age. In her place as a simple believer, but first among the faithful because she is their mother. She lends support to the common prayer, and with the Apostles and the other disciples adds her voice in imploring the gift of the Holy Spirit, that same Spirit who had overshadowed her at the Annunciation and made her the Mother of God.

The Annunciation and Pentecost: here are two moments which are mysteriously perpetuated in the Church: what happened at Nazareth, what was done in the Upper Room, takes place each day on all the altars in the world: it is thus that "the Spirit of the Lord has filled the universe."

Beloved people of Milan, these are the thoughts that today's Solemnity of Pentecost suggests to us as we are assembled in this historic Piazza del Duomo (Cathedral Square), watched over by the Madonnina, with its thousand pinnacles rising to heaven like hands in prayer. This monument, famous symbol of the faith and civilization of Milan, re-awakens memories and affections that bind me to this Lombardy capital, having come here often and for different reasons. How can one deny knowing one of the cities that has experienced Christianity in depth right from the time of the great Bishop Ambrose? In Milan St. Augustine heard his first call to the faith and began his prestigious doctrinal and pastoral teaching.

There is yet a personal reason that ideally places me in your midst: my name a Karol, Charles, and my parents, in giving me this name, wanted to entrust me to the protection of St. Charles Borromeo. Finally, I wish to recall with particular affection one who was Archbishop of Milan, namely, my predecessor Paul VI. If for me he was a teacher, he was for you and among you a provident and enlightened spiritual leader. The common emotion that you and I feel in recalling his memory is likewise a bond and a sign of sincere friendship.

In recalling these events, episodes and circumstances that now belong to the past, but which have been linked to one another by a mysterious Marian thread, as though in preparation and as a seal of this solemn meeting that is taking place under the gaze of the Most Holy Virgin, let us raise our hearts to her and invoke her as the Queen of Heaven and Earth. To her and to her motherly protection we entrust all those killed in the tragic disaster yesterday on the Autostrada dei Fiori. Let us pray for the speedy recovery of the injured; let us implore comfort for the families stricken by so much sorrow. May our heavenly Mother help and console everyone.

* * *

In this reflection on two great mysteries, the Annunciation and Pentecost, the Holy Father fills five short paragraphs with many thoughts. To help clarify what he says, may we first simply list the ways he sees Mary's cooperation with the Holy Spirit.

1. Mary was predisposed by the grace of the Redeemer.
2. Mary responded in obedience to every request of God.
3. Mary consecrated her virginity to the Lord.
4. She was attentive to the needs of others.
5. She was dedicated to the mission and person of Jesus.
6. She was the perfect disciple of Christ.
7. She shared in the sacrifice of Jesus.
8. The Spirit gradually enlightened her faith.
9. The Spirit revealed to her the work and the Word of her Son.
10. The Spirit supported her on Calvary.
11. The Spirit fashioned Mary in glory.

    Mary on her part responded to the action of the Spirit:

12. By praying with the Apostles in the Upper Room.

13. By praying with the Church in every age.
14. By believing.
15. By being first among believers because she is the mother of Jesus.

Finally, the Pope reminds us that what had happened in Nazareth and what had happened in the Upper Room, happens as well at each celebration of the Eucharist.

*May 29, 1983*

# Mary's Communion with the Trinity

## "Glory to the Father and to the Son and to the Holy Spirit."

This Sunday the liturgy has us meditate on the central truth of Christianity: the Most Holy Trinity. Jesus has revealed to us the secrets of divine life and its manifestation in the world, announcing that the one God is three equal and distinct Persons: the Father, creator of heaven and earth; the Son, who became incarnate for the salvation of man; and the Holy Spirit, who proceeds form the Father and the Son, for building up the Church and carrying out every work of sanctification.

In this meeting for prayer, we wish to combine the adoration of this mystery with the veneration of that creature to whom it was granted more than to any other to know it and, we could say, to have an intimate experience of it: Mary, the Mother of God. Indeed, the Virgin's communion with the three Divine Persons is very special and unique: made fruitful by the Holy Spirit, she is the Mother of the Incarnate

---

From *L'Osservatore Romano* No. 23 (787) 6 June 1983
Title: "Mary's Communion with the Trinity is Most Special"

Word, and so her Son is the same Son of the Father. Who more than she, therefore, is close to the Most Holy Trinity? What creature more than she can help us know the Trinity and love it?

If the Church, as the Second Vatican Council says, "is a people made one with the unity of the Father, the Son, and the Holy Spirit" (*Lumen Gentium,* 4), and Mary is the Mother of the Church, this means that only through her motherly intercession can we understand ever better how the Spirit constitutes, preserves and perfects the unity of the Church, leading it, in history, to the fullness of truth.

The Holy Virgin is the chosen dwelling of the Most Holy Trinity, the temple where its glory dwells (cf. Ps 26:8). It is she who obtains from her Son, that we too are temples of God, inhabited and moved by the Spirit of the Lord (cf. 1Cor 3:16). It is thanks to her prayer that the Church grows "fitted together as a holy temple in the Lord" (Eph 2:21).

* * *

1. The works of God which relate in any way to creation are the works of the one LORD GOD. It is through Jesus that this LORD GOD is revealed to us as a Trinity of Persons, Father, Son and Holy Spirit. We may know what each of these words mean but when we put them together, we do not know. It is a mystery, the mystery of the Trinity. To help us enter this mystery in some small way, the Holy Father attributes to the Father, Son and Holy Spirit, different aspects of creation.

2. In all of creation, there is no one more intimately related to the Trinity than Mary. Her experience of the Trinity is so intimate that the Pope uses the word "communion"—in union with—to describe it.

3. After the message of the Angel at the Annunciation, the Virgin Mary was made fruitful by the overshadowing of the Holy Spirit. Her Son Jesus is the Word of the Father from all eternity.

4. Quoting the Second Vatican Council to the effect that the unity of the Church is the work of the Spirit, the Pope suggests that

as we reflect on the work of the Holy Spirit in Mary, we may better be able to see the work of the Holy Spirit in the Church.

5. As we are close to Mary and she is united to Christ, so we too are united with Him and become temples of the Lord.

*June 5, 1983*

# The Eucharist and the Blessed Virgin Mary

"Ave verum Corpus natum de Maria Virgine!" Hail, true Body born of the Virgin Mary! On the feast of the Most Holy Body and Blood of Christ, our grateful thanks is raised to the Father who has given us the Divine Word, the living Bread come down from heaven, and our thanks is joyfully raised to the Virgin, who offered the Lord his innocent Flesh and his precious Blood which we receive at the altar.

"*Ave, verum Corpus*": true Body, truly conceived through the work of the Holy Spirit, borne in the womb with ineffable love (Preface II of Advent), born for us of the Virgin Mary: "*natum de Maria Virgine.*"

The divine Body and Blood, which after the consecration is present on the Altar, is offered to the Father. It becomes Communion of love for everyone, by consolidating us in the unity of the Spirit in order to found the Church, and preserves its maternal origin from Mary. She prepared that Body and Blood before offering them to the Word as a gift from the whole human family that he might be clothed in them in becoming our Redeemer, High Priest and Victim.

At the root of the Eucharist, therefore, there is the virginal

---

From *L'Osservatore Romano* No. 24 (788) 13 June 1983
Title: "At the Root of the Eucharist is the Virginal and Maternal Life of Mary"

and maternal life of Mary, her overflowing experience of God, her journey of faith and love, which through the work of the Holy Spirit made her a temple and her heart an altar: because she conceived not according to nature, but through faith, with a free and conscious act: an act of obedience. And if the Body that we eat and the Blood that we drink is the inestimable gift of the Risen Lord to us travelers, it still has in itself, as fragrant Bread, the taste and aroma of the Virgin Mother.

*"Vere passum, immolatum in Cruce pro homine."*

> That Body truly suffered and was immolated on the Cross for man.

Born of the Virgin to be a pure, holy and immaculate oblation, Christ offered on the Cross the one perfect Sacrifice which every Mass, in an unbloody manner, renews and makes present. In that one Sacrifice, Mary, the first redeemed, the Mother of the Church, had an active part. She stood near the Crucified, suffering deeply with her Firstborn; with a motherly heart she associated herself with his Sacrifice: with love she consented to his immolation (cf. *Lumen Gentium,* 58; *Marialis Cultus,* 20): she offered him and she offered herself to the Father. Every Eucharist is a memorial of that Sacrifice and that Passover that restored life to the world; every Mass puts us in intimate communion with her, the mother, whose sacrifice "becomes present" just as the Sacrifice of her Son "becomes present" at the words of consecration of the bread and wine pronounced by the priest (cf. Discourse at the Celebration of the Word 2 June 1983, n.2).

* * *

1. Using the text of the hymn *Ave Verum* the Holy Father composes a counterpoint of the different facets of our faith as it relates to the Blessed Sacrament and Our Lady.

2. We give thanks to the Father for the gift of the Word, the Living Bread from Heaven, and then we joyfully thank Mary who offered the Lord his Flesh and Blood.

3. The Body of Christ was conceived by the Holy Spirit and now this same Body was carried in the womb of the Virgin Mary.

4. The Body and Blood are offered to the Father and become Communion for each of us. Mary offered the Body and Blood prepared in her as a gift to the Father from all humanity.

5. The whole life of Mary is recalled as we share in the gift of the risen Lord;

her virginal and maternal life,
her overflowing experience of God,
her journey of faith and love,
her body as a temple, her heart as an altar,
her free and conscious conception in faith,
her obedience.

6. Pope John Paul II offers a second set of counterpoints as he reflects on the Mass;

Christ offered the one perfect sacrifice while Mary stood by his Cross.
Christ renews and makes present this sacrifice in each Mass while Mary continues her consent to his immolation as she likewise offers him to the Father.

7. Each Mass is a memorial of that Sacrifice which restores life to the world. In every Mass we are put in intimate communion with her whose sacrifice is indeed "made present."

*June 12, 1983*

# Mary Teaches Us to Pray

In many environments, and especially in youth movements, we notice today a rediscovery of the value of prayer. There is a rediscovery of the profoundly human and biblical meaning of prayer: that is, putting oneself in contact with God, being open to his will for oneself and for others, finding oneself, without any illusions, radically poor before divine infinite richness. At these privileged moments one can understand, as St. Catherine of Siena used to say, that we do not have our existence "from ourselves," but we have it "from he who is."

Prayer is one of the sublime activities of the saints in the Kingdom of Heaven, beginning with Christ, the Holy One of God.

The New Testament assures us that Jesus continues to pray and to intercede for us with the Father (Jn 14:16;1 Jn 2:1; Rom 8:34). The Letter to the Hebrews makes it clear that Jesus "is always able to save those who approach God through him, since he forever lives to make intercession for them" (Heb 7:25).

This praying and salvific attitude of Christ does not exclude but rather demands the prayer of the faithful and of the

---

From *L'Osservatore Romano* No. 25 (789) 20 June 1983
Title: "Let Us Always Remember that Mary Is Praying for Us"

saints, who in union with him must implore the graces of salvation for themselves and for others.

What wonderful divine disposition! Prayer illuminates and sustains the course of history and the destiny of the brethren! It is a sign of the solidarity of men and the mutual help they can offer one another whenever they put themselves at the disposal of God's plans!

But what creature is more at the Lord's disposal than Mary, his Mother and Handmaid? Who more than she continues in heaven to praise, adore and entreat the Lord? She, states the Second Vatican Council, "taken up to heaven, did not lay aside this saving role, but by her manifold acts of intercession continues to win for us the gifts of eternal salvation" (*Lumen Gentium,* 62).

Yes, Mary is the great pray-er. She extends her hands in gesture of openness to God and of universal entreaty, maternally concerned about the salvation of everyone.

Let us always remember that in heaven Mary is praying for us, and let us therefore confidently rely on her powerful intercession, with the desire that God's will may be done in us.

To the protection and the intercession of Mary, as well as to your prayers, I entrust the pilgrimage that, God willing, I will undertake to Poland next Thursday on the occasion of the six-hundredth anniversary of the image of Our Lady of Jasna Gora.

May God bless this pastoral initiative and have it bear abundant fruits for the good of the Church and for the whole population of the dear Polish nation.

* * *

1. In this message about prayer, the Holy Father expresses his joy that many people are rediscovering what prayer is and just how important it is. In rediscovering prayer, we are able to rediscover ourselves. We have our existence, our being, from the Lord.

2. What is prayer? It is, he says:

(a) putting oneself in contact with God,
(b) being open to His will for oneself and for others,
(c) finding oneself radically poor before the divine richness,
(d) one of the sublime activities of the saints,
(e) the intercession of Jesus with the Father for us,
(f) the response of the faithful who are in union with Jesus.

3. The effects of prayer are:

(a) the illumination of history,
(b) to sustain the course of history,
(c) to be a sign of solidarity and of mutual help in working out God's plan of salvation.

4. Relating both the nature of prayer and its effect to Mary, the Holy Father reminds us that:

(a) no one was more disposed to do God's will than she,
(b) no one was more faithful to the praise, adoration and entreaty to God than she,
(c) no one more than she continues to win the gifts of eternal salvation for us.

5. Mary is preeminently a "pray-er," one who prays. She shows this:

(a) in her openness to God,
(b) in her universal intercession,
(c) in her maternal concern for all.

6. The Pope then asks for Mary's protection and our prayers as he begins his pilgrimage to his native Poland.

*June 19, 1983*
*In Czestochowa*

# The Angelus: The Beginning of the Redemption

Before finishing Mass, I wish now to recite the Angelus, just as I recite this prayer at noon every Sunday in Rome. The Angelus expresses all the eloquence of the Mystery that, among other things, has given origin to the Polish sanctuary at Jasna Gora: as the humble handmaid of the Lord, Mary accepted the Archangel's announcement, and through the power of the Holy Spirit became the Mother of the Eternal Word. "The Word became flesh and dwelt among us" (Jn 1:14), in order to accomplish the Redemption of the world.

The Angelus prayer records for us the beginning of the mystery of Redemption in which we are especially seeking to be immersed during this year of Extraordinary Jubilee.

* * *

1. This message was given at Jasna Gora at the shrine of Our Lady of Czestochowa on the occasion of the Pope's pilgrimage to Poland in 1983.

2. The year 1983 was a "Jubilee Year," a time of special prayer and indulgence to mark the 1950th anniversary of the death of

---

From *L'Osservatore Romano* No. 26 (790) 27 June 1983
Title: "The Angelus Records the Beginning of the Mystery of the Redemption"

Jesus for the redemption of humankind. The Angelus, the Pope reminds us, marks the beginning of this mystery.

3. As we pray the Angelus, we meditate as well on the revelation of God's eternal plan of love for us.

4. Also on this occasion the Holy Father spoke at some length to various types of working people in Poland congratulating them on their work. We have omitted these exhortations from our reflection.

*June 26, 1983*

# Mary Prefigured in the Old Testament

On my return from my pilgrimage to Poland, I address, above all, cordial greetings to you dear Romans and to you pilgrims here present, thanking you for the prayers with which you accompanied my apostolic journey among the people of my homeland.

In the Sanctuary of Jasna Gora I prayed intensely for the dear Diocese of Rome and for all Christian communities: I invoked Mary's motherly protection for the whole Church entrusting to her its growth in faith, hope and love.

Today, meditating on the Angelus prayer, we will begin a new series of reflections that will have as a theme the prefigurement of Mary in the Old Testament.

The Second Vatican Council attributes to Our Lady the title of "exalted Daughter of Sion."[1] It is a name that owes its origin to the traditions of the Old Testament and is an expression of strictly Eastern flavor.

Sion, in fact, was the stronghold of ancient Jerusalem. It was to this summit that King David had the Ark of the Covenant brought,[2] and his son Solomon built the Temple there.[3] Since then, the mountain of the Temple has been designated above all by the name Sion.[4] Sion, therefore, was

---

From *L'Osservatore Romano* No. 27 (791) 4 July 1983
Title: "Mary Prefigured in the Old Testament"

the heart of Jerusalem, the most sacred part of the Holy City, since there the Lord dwelt in his house. As such, the hill of Sion came to designate all Jerusalem[5] and even all Israel,[6] of which Jerusalem was both the religious and the political center.

Mary can be called "Daughter of Sion" inasmuch as the vocation of ancient Jerusalem and of the entire Chosen People finds its culmination and concrete expression in her. She is the flower of Israel, opened up at the end of a long itinerary made up of lights and shadows, during which God was preparing Israel to receive the Messiah. In Mary of Nazareth, God fulfilled in advance the promises made to Abraham and his descendants.

According to many exegetes, in the Angel Gabriel's words to Mary there is heard the echo of that joyful message that the prophets had addressed to the Daughter of Sion. Indeed, Mary is invited to rejoice ("Rejoice, O highly favored daughter"),[7] because the Son of God will take up his dwelling in her.[8] He will be the King and Savior of the new house of Jacob[9] which is the Church.

As the "Daughter of Sion," the Virgin is therefore the point of arrival of the Old Testament and the first fruits of the Church. She is consequently a permanent reminder to recall the bonds that tie us to Abraham, "our Father in faith,"[10] and to the people who hoped for and awaited the event of the Redemption. She is furthermore an admonition that the Church—the new "Daughter of Sion"—live in joy.[11] In the face of the emergencies of our pilgrimage we must tremble, yes, but we must not fear like "people of little faith."[12] Christ is the "Powerful One who saves us from selfishness and coldheartedness. In shedding his blood he takes possession of us as King, so that every creature may attain the perfect measure of love.

**NOTES**

1. "Lumen Gentium", 55.
2. 2 Sam 6
3. 2 Sam 24:16–25(cf. 2 Chr 3:1); 1Kgs 6
4. Is 18:7; Jer 26,18; Ps 2:6;48:2–3
5. Is 37:32; 51:1; Jer 26:18; 51:35; Zep 3:16
6. Is 46:13; Ps 149:2
7. Lk 1:28
8. Lk 1:31–32a
9. Lk 1:32b–33
10. Eucharistic Prayer I
11. cf. Phil 4:4
12. Mt 8:26 and parallels in Mk 4:40 and Lk 8:25

* * *

1. When Jesus spoke with the disciples on the way to Emmaus and "interpreted to them what referred to him in all the Scriptures . . ." (Lk 24:27), He was using the Hebrew Scriptures, the Old Testament. On this Sunday the Holy Father begins a series of reflections in which he will study these Scriptures with the eyes of Faith and help us to see things which we may not have seen before.

2. "Sion" was the religious and political center of Israel and quite properly we may call Mary "Daughter of Sion." In her the vocation of the Chosen People finds its fulfillment. She is the first of the children of Abraham to receive the Messiah.

3. The Lord had often revealed to Israel the joy of the coming Messiah. As we listen carefully to the message of the Angel to Mary at the Annunciation, we can hear an echo of these revelations. An "exegete" is a biblical scholar.

4. We must never forget how important Mary is as a permanent reminder of how closely we are bound to the children of Abraham. Both the Jewish people and we ourselves look upon him as "our father in faith."

5. Faith generates fortitude, and the faith of Mary is for us an example of how to conduct ourselves during the course of our earthly pilgrimage. We are a people of faith united with Christ.

*July 3, 1983*

# Mary's "Fiat" Is the Fulfillment of Israel's Covenant

Mary's "fiat" at the Annunciation allows God to inaugurate a New Covenant with mankind, even more wonderful than the one ratified with the people of Israel.

We recall an occasion on a day long ago, yet so exalting, when the Lord, at the foot of Mt. Sinai, proposed to the tribes of Israel the offering of his Covenant of love through the Prophet Moses, his spokesman.

This is what God said to the people: "You have seen for yourselves how I treated the Egyptians and how I bore you up on eagle wings and brought you here to myself. Therefore if you hearken to my voice and keep my covenant, you shall be my special possession, dearer to me than all other people, though all the earth is mine. You shall be to be a kingdom of priests, a holy nation."[1]

Moses then explained to his brothers and sisters the content of the divine message; he instructed them in order to make them aware that the plan that came from the Lord God, even if it was a command, did no violence to their free will. He who created his children free is the most jealous guardian of their freedom.

---

From *L'Osservatore Romano* No. 28 (792) 11 July 1983
Title: "Mary's FIAT the Fulfillment of Israel's FIAT on Sinai"

After being enlightened by Moses' teachings, all the people answered as one: "Everything the Lord has said, we will do!"[2] These words, which will remain memorable in the Jewish spirituality of every age, were like the "fiat," that is, the "yes," with which Israel accepted its being united to Yahweh its God, as a bride to her husband.

In the light of these facts, we can perhaps better understand the scene of the Annunciation. The Angel Gabriel, sent by God, reveals to the Virgin the plan that the Lord has for her: to give birth to the Son of God himself, who will become King and Savior of the new People of God,[3] the Church. It is a new form of the Covenant. This time God asks to be united to us by taking on our very features.

Mary, in the face of the divine proposal, behaves knowingly and freely. If God is asking her, then she too asks her God: "How can this be, since I do not know man?"[4] The angel offers further enlightenment about the divine will: "The Holy Spirit will come upon you . . ."[5]

Through being called to believe the unbelievable, Mary at this point exclaims: "I am the servant of the Lord. Let it be done to me as you say."[6]

In these words of the Virgin, there is substantially the echo of those words spoken by the entire people of Israel when they accepted the gift of the Covenant on Sinai. And this means that the faith of Israel matured on Mary's lips. Truly she is "Daughter of Sion!"

We will now call to mind Mary's "fiat" as we pray the Angelus. Let us ask the Virgin to make the "fiat" of our Baptism always enlightened and generous, and to renew it in the daily commitments of our witness of faith. Thus we will live worthily of our Covenant with the Lord in his Church, the heart of the world.

**NOTES**

1. Ex 19:4–6a
2. Ex 19:8; cf. 24:3,7
3. Lk 1:31–33.
4. Lk 1:34
5. Lk 1:35
6. Lk 1:38a

* * *

1. A person of faith can see things that others cannot see and hear things which others cannot hear. It is in faith that the Holy Father asks us to go back to that scene which we can recall so vividly: when Moses came down from Mt. Sinai to give the people of Israel the Ten Commandments. As we re-read the 19th Chapter of the Book of Exodus, we are reminded that Moses did much more than just "give" them the commandments.

2. The Pope reminds us of something which we frequently overlook. The covenant with the people of Israel was a covenant of love. God chooses his people freely and makes this gift to them: they will be his people and he will be their God.

3. The crucial point is the acceptance of the covenant by the people. "Whatever the Lord has said, we will do." We are ready to do the will of the Lord. This assent is central to Jewish spirituality even to this day.

4. Now the Pope moves our focus to the scene at Nazareth. Here the angel reveals God's plan to Mary and asks for her assent. She shows that she is free. She questions the messenger! She shows that she is willing. She speaks her "fiat!" Her consent is likewise central to Christian spirituality to this day.

5. What was spoken in faith and obedience by the people of Israel in the desert comes to its fullness when pronounced by Mary, the true "Daughter of Sion."

6. Now the Holy Father makes one more important observation. The assent to the Covenant was not made just by Mary, but by each one of us at our baptism and is renewed in our daily lives.

# Ark of the Covenant

Christian piety honors the holy Virgin with the title of "Ark of the Covenant," a title which comes from a great distance.

The sacred books of the Old Testament continually express the joyful certainty: God is in the midst of his people; he has chosen Israel as his dwelling place.

The Lord's Dwelling among the people of his election is intimately connected with the covenant which he wanted to establish on Mount Sinai. It is as if to say that God makes himself so "allied," that is, near, a friend and in solidarity with man, that he wants to be always with us. He himself declares: "I will set my Dwelling among you, and will not disdain you. Ever present in your midst, I will be your God and you will be my people."[1]

The Covenant having just been entered on the slopes of Sinai, the people, on God's order,[2] erected the so-called Meeting Tent in which there was the Ark, called "of the Covenant": in fact it contained the two tables on which were inscribed the Ten Commandments given to Moses by the Lord.[3] The Ark, as the tangible sign of God's presence, was to accompany the people along their wandering in the desert, right up to their settling in Palestine. Then, as a work of Solomon, the Temple of Jerusalem was built. In its most

From *L'Osservatore Romano* No. 29 (793) 18 July 1983
Title: "Ark of the Covenant"

secret part, called the "Holy of Holies," the Ark was placed.[4] That was the most sacred place in all of Israel. Within that enclosure, in symbolic form, the Lord dwelled. To represent this Dwelling of God in the heart of his people, the religious language of the Old Testament frequently uses the image of the "cloud." With the use of this figurative element, the sacred books speak of God who comes down to dwell on Mount Sinai,[5] in the Meeting Tent[6] and in the Temple of Jerusalem.[7]

And here we are at an unexpected change. When the Angel Gabriel made the announcement to Mary, God revealed to this maiden his intention to leave his Dwelling in the Temple of Jerusalem in order to establish another form of dwelling among his people, that is, he wanted to be united to us by making himself one of us, taking on our countenance.

Mary, enveloped by the mystical cloud of the Holy Spirit, gives her assent to God's plan. From that moment her womb becomes the Ark of the New Covenant, the holy sanctuary where the Incarnate Presence of God came down to dwell.

As the Ark which bears in itself the Lord made flesh, Mary is the type of every believer. Indeed, each one of us, when we welcome the Word of God by uttering our "fiat," makes his own person the sanctuary of the divine indwelling. Jesus assures us of this when he says: "Anyone who loves me will be true to my word, and my Father will love him; we will come to him and make our dwelling place with him."[8]

**NOTES**

1. Lev 26:11,12
2. cf. Ex 25:8
3. Ex 25;16;31:18;Deut 10:1–5
4. 1 Kgs 8:1–13
5. Ex 24:16

6. Ex 40:34–35
7. 1 Kgs 8:10–12; cf. 2 Chr 5:15
8. Jn 14:25

* * *

1. Reading the Scriptures with the eyes of faith allows us to focus on incidents and events in Jewish history which find their fulfillment in Christ. It is for this reason that the Holy Father spends some time in establishing the details of the Ark as the sign of the presence of the Lord among us. It is helpful to reread the Scripture citations he gives.

2. The Lord gave Israel a tangible sign of his presence when he instructed them to build the Ark. Within the Ark were the tablets of the Commandments, the staff of Moses and some of the manna from the desert. Each was a sign of the nearness of the Lord and his care for his People.

3. The Ark was to be placed in the Meeting-Tent, the tabernacle. Later the Lord would fill the tabernacle with a "cloud" as a sign of his "Dwelling" among his people.

4. Later when the Temple was built by Solomon, the Ark was placed in the Holy of Holies and once again the Temple was filled, overshadowed, by the "cloud," the sign of the presence of God (1 Kings 8).

5. In the account of the Annunciation, the Angel Gabriel reveals God's plan to Mary. Then, in response to her question, the angel assures her that "The Holy Spirit will come upon you and the power of the Most High will overshadow you" (Lk 1:35).

6. With Mary, the Lord dwells among us in the flesh. He has become one with us as one like us. The Lord is now really present with us and not as a sign.

7. The Holy Father reminds us that there is more to our faith than merely knowing what has happened. Each one of us has also spoken a "fiat" when we made our baptismal promises and live up to them. We love Jesus. God comes to us and dwells within us.

# Mary's Spiritual Testament

"Do whatever he tell you."[1] With these words, the Mother of Jesus, present at the wedding that was being celebrated one day in Cana of Galilee,[2] suggested to the banquet waiters that they do what Jesus would order them.

The spirituality of the Old Testament can put us on the path to determining the remote origin of this exhortation of Mary.

On Mount Sinai, in fact, the Lord, through Moses, invited the people of Israel to enter his covenant.[3] In response to the divine offer, all the people exclaimed in one voice: "Everything the Lord has said, we will do."[4]

It can be affirmed that every generation of the Chosen People remembered that ready declaration of obedience made "on the day of the assembly"[5] at the foot of Sinai. Thinking back on it, Israel loved to rediscover the freshness of the first love.[6] In fact, the content of the same phrase was repeated regularly every time the people, guided by their leaders, renewed the obligations of the Sinai Covenant throughout the history of the Old Testament.[7]

"Now," commented my venerable predecessor Paul VI in his Apostolic Exhortation *Marialis Cultus,*[8] "the words that the Virgin spoke to the servants at the marriage feast of Cana

---

From *L'Osservatore Romano* No. 30 (794), 25 July 1983
Title: "Mary's Spiritual Testament"

which at first sight were limited to the desire to remedy an embarrassment at the feast, are seen in the context of St. John's Gospel to re-echo the words used by the people of Israel to give approval to the Covenant,[9] and to renew their commitments.[10] And they are words which harmonize wonderfully with those spoken by the Father at the theophany on Mount Tabor: "Listen to him!"[11]

Today, the servants at the marriage are we, dear brothers and sisters. The Virgin does not cease to repeat to each one of us, her sons and daughters, what she said at Cana. That advice could be called her spiritual testament. It is, in fact, the last word that the Gospels have given us from her, the Holy Mother. Let us accept it and keep it in our hearts!

**NOTES**

1. Jn 2:5
2. Jn 2:1–12
3. Ex 18:3–7
4. Ex 19:8; cf. 24:5,7
5. Dt 4:10
6. cf. Jer 2:2; Hos 2:17
7. Jos 24:24; Ezr 10:12; Neh 5:12 . . .
8. 2 February 1974 (*Acta Sancta Sede* 6,1974,pp.166–67,n.57).
9. Ex 19:8;24:5,7; Dt 5:27.
10. Jos 24:24; Ezr 10:12; Neh 5:12.
11. Mt.17:5

* * *

1. The Holy Father here uses a tool which Scripture itself teaches us to use. Both Testaments, Hebrew and Christian, share a common heritage, language and spirituality. In this reflection, therefore, the words of Mary found in St. John's Gospel have their meaning amplifed through their Hebrew origins.

2. The Gospels are not simple history, they are "theology," the study of God revealing God to us. Thus in St. John's Gospel, the events which happened at Cana were not the account of a miracle

Jesus worked to avoid an embarrassment. Rather we can see an important revelation from God.

3. To understand a little better what really happened at Cana we must go back to Mount Sinai and to the invitation to become God's chosen people which was offered to the Hebrews. Their response was "Whatever the Lord asks of us, we will do."

4. After the Exile when Jerusalem was being restored, Ezra exhorted the people to fidelity to the Covenant. They also responded with a variation of this same theme. "Whatever the Lord asks, we will do."

5. The word "theophany" means a visible manifestation of the presence of God. It is very close in meaning to the word "epiphany,"—God revealing himself to us. The Father has the same message for us: listen to his Son.

6. All that the Pope has said is the setting—is context. Now we see much deeper into the mystery revealed here.

7. We may not have reflected on it before, but it is interesting to note that these are the last words of Mary recorded in the Scriptures. They are in fact her spiritual testament to us.

*July 24, 1983*

# Mary Remembers the Words and Deeds of Jesus

"Mary treasured all these things and reflected on them in her heart" (Lk 2:19; cf. 2:51). So does the Evangelist Luke attest to Mary's contemplation, which preserved the memory of Jesus' infancy. Even in this, the Virgin shows that she inherited the faith of ancient Israel, asked by God to "recall in its heart" all that he had done on their behalf.

We must note, however, that the purpose of "memory," according to the Bible, is essentially dynamic, actualizing: it pushes ahead. And the reason is this: What God brought about in the past to help his people is a guarantee that he will act in the same way in the present circumstances and in the future (cf.Dt 7:17–21), since his love is eternal and unchangeable (Ps 136:1 ff.). Therefore Mary Most Holy, too, with regard to the words and deeds of Jesus, exercised an active memory. On the one hand she "preserves" the remembrance of those words and deeds; on the other, however, the intellect strives to examine them, "reflecting on them" (Lk 2:19: Greek *symballousa*), trying to understand their proper meaning and give them an exact interpretation.

The Church too, imitates Mary's example by ceaselessly recalling what her Lord said and did. The Apostle Paul left

From *L'Osservatore Romano* No. 31 (795) 1 August 1983
Title: "Like Mary, the Church Reflects on Christ's Words and Deeds"

this charge to his disciple Timothy: "Remember that Jesus Christ, a descendant of David, was raised from the dead. This is the Gospel I preach . . . Guard the rich deposit of faith with the help of the Holy Spirit who dwells within us" (2 Tim 2:8;1:14).

The Eucharist is the especial expression of this memorial of the teaching and the example of Jesus. "Do this as a remembrance of me" (Lk 22:19; 1 Cor 11:24,25). In the Eucharist we listen to and recall the Saviour's Word so that, renewed by his Spirit, we may live it in the changeable circumstances of our history.

* * *

1. Memory is not simply nostalgia. Nostalgia simply grieves of the past which is gone. Memory, rather, is an active power. It has the power to make an event present once again. The event may have taken place in the past but memory has the power to allow that event to affect me in the present.

2. Jewish Prayer each day recalls the saving deeds of the Lord in the course of its long history. The memory of the Lord's mercy from those past times is the guarantee that the mercy of the Lord will continue.

3. So too, when Mary remembers, it is to recall the words and deeds of Jesus. More importantly, however, it is to make them present once again and to discern their proper meaning and their exact interpretation.

4. It is the same with St. Paul's admonition to Timothy. Immediately before the verse quoted by the Pope, St. Paul had said to Timothy: "Reflect on what I am saying, for the Lord will give you understanding in everything" (2 Tim 2:7).

5. The supreme example of the power of remembrance is in the Eucharist. Jesus told us to celebrate in remembrance of him. When we do, He himself is made present as our help and guide in today's world.

*July 31, 1983*

# Mary Our Model in Time of Trial

When Mary and Joseph found the Child Jesus in the Temple after three days of anxious search, his mother was unable to restrain this loving complaint: "Son, why have you treated us so? Behold your father and I have been looking for you anxiously" (Lk 2:48).

It is comforting for us to know that even Our Lady asked "why" of Jesus, on an occasion of intense suffering. We recognize in her words what had already been a constant theme in the books of the Old Testament.

From those venerable pages we learn how frequently the People of God, or some of its members, passed through crucial trials.

In similar difficulties a question arises: "My God, my God, why hast thou forsaken me?" (Ps 22:2)—"Why sleepest thou, O Lord?" . . . why dost thou hide they face, forgetting our affliction and oppression?" (Ps 44,24,25). In response to this very human "why," one who prays the Psalms turns to Israel's past, meditating again on the history of the Father, especially the Exodus from Egypt, and drawing from it the following lesson: they also were tried as gold in a furnace, but the Lord saved them in so many ways and often by unexpected paths; and because the Lord is faithful, even now he

From *L'Osservatore Romano* No. 32 (796) 8 August 1983
Title: "May Respect for Human Rights Prevail"

will grant salvation in the manner and at the time which pleases him (Ps 22,5–6; Sir 2,10;51,8; Jud 8,15–17,26).

"Thus the Blessed Virgin—the Second Vatican Council teaches—advanced on her pilgrimage of faith, and loyally persevered in her union with her Son unto the Cross" (*Lumen Gentium,* 58).

The episode of the finding in the temple shows that she was not able at all times and at once to understand the conduct of her Son. As a matter of fact, Luke notes that she as well as Joseph did not understand Jesus' reply (Lk 2:50). In spite of this, however, Mary "kept all these things in her heart" (Lk 2:51).

Then come the days when Jesus foretells his death and resurrection as a design spoken of in the Scriptures (Lk 9:22,43–45; 18:31–33;24:6–7,26–27).

She, surely, as a true "daughter of Sion" will watch over the sorrowful mission of her Son with the resources which came to her through faith (cf. Lk 11:27–28). If God, in the vicissitudes of his people, had so many times loosed the chains of the just suffering tribulations, he can even now bring to fulfillment the promise that Christ should rise from the dead (cf. Heb 11:19; Rom 4:17).

Mary's attitude inspires our faith. When tempests rage and all seems lost, the remembrance of what the Lord has done in the past sustains us. Let us recall, above all, the death and resurrection of Jesus; and then the innumerable liberations which Christ has effected in the history of the Church, in the world, and in the hearts of individual believers.

From this recollection there will spring forth a more fruitful and joyous certainty that even at the present time, however threatening, the Redeemer sails with us in the same ship. And the wind and the sea obey him (cf. Mk 4:41; Mt 8:27; Lk 8:25).

* * *

1. There is one type of prayer with which Christians in general feel somewhat uncomfortable. It is the prayer in which we question the Lord. So it is a surprise and a little disconcerting to hear Mary ask Jesus "Why have you caused such suffering?"

2. This prayer form is used frequently in the Hebrew Scriptures and in Jewish practice. The Holy Father quotes the most notable of these, especially the Psalm which Jesus used as he hung on the Cross.

3. To question the Lord is not a sign of doubt or even of disobedience, but rather of profound trust. Even as they question the Lord, they know deep down, that the Lord is faithful.

4. We know that Mary asked Jesus "why" after he had been lost in Jerusalem and we may surmise that she may have asked the same question of him as he foretold his death and as he hung on the Cross.

5. In a previous message (July 24), the Holy Father has reminded us that memory makes present the past event. So in this case, the remembrance of Mary's sorrows sustains our faith and brings joy to the world. After all, even the wind and the sea obey him.

*August 7, 1983*
*At Castel Gandolfo*

# Mary, Mother of Church Unity

The impulse which the Second Vatican Council has given to the ecumenical movement makes us raise our glance to Mary, "Mother of unity" and "Mother of the dispersed children of God."

In the Old Testament the "dispersed children of God" are the exiles in a foreign land, especially in Babylonia. The Lord permitted their dispersion among the peoples because of their sins (Dt 4:25–27;28:62–66), but once they were converted by the preaching of the prophets (Dt 4:29–31; 30:1–6), God gathers them together from the diaspora and makes them return to their own country.

The Temple of Jerusalem, reconstructed from the ruins, is the privileged place of this reunification (Ex 37:21,26–28: 2 Mac 1:27–29). Beneath its vaults the converts who had become members of a new Covenant, adore the same Lord; and Jerusalem becomes "the universal mother" of these numberless sons whom Yahweh, her Spouse, brought together within her walls (Is 49:21;60:1–9; Ps 87; Tob 13:11–13). That surrounding wall, in effect, resembles a womb which contains the Temple and all those who assemble there to adore the One God.

It is especially the Evangelist John who in the light of the

---

From *L'Osservatore Romano* No. 33 (797) 13 August 1983
Title: "Mary, Mother of the Unity of the Church"

Redemption carried out by Christ treats of these themes prepared from the Old Covenant.

Jesus, by his death, is the one who gathers together in unity the dispersed children of God (Jn 11:51–52). The "dispersed" nowadays are all men, inasmuch as they are victims of the evil one who snatches and scatters (Jn 10:12). They, however, can become "children of God," if they accept Christ and his Word (Jn 1:12; 1 Jn 5:1). And Christ gathers together dispersed humanity in another Temple, that is, his own person, which reveals the Father and brings mankind to perfect union with him (Jn 10:30; 17:21).

And the "true Jerusalem" is formed from the flock of his disciples, that is, the Church, into which Jesus leads Jews and Gentiles (Jn 10:16; 11:51–52; 12:32–33). Of this new Jerusalem, Mary is the Mother. "Behold your sons gathered together," says the prophet to the ancient Jerusalem (Is 60:4). "Woman, behold your Son," Jesus says to his Mother, when from the Cross he entrusts her to the beloved disciple (Jn 19:26), who represented all his disciples of every age.

Sensitive, therefore, to the ecumenical prompting of the Council and in communion with our brothers of the World Council of Churches in Vancouver, we entreat the Mother of God and of men that "all families of peoples . . . may be happily gathered together in peace and harmony into one People of God for the glory of the Most Holy and Undivided Trinity" (*Lumen Gentium,* 69).

Yesterday, the 6th of August, feast of the Transfiguration of the Lord, we recalled the unforgettable figure of my beloved predecessor Paul VI, five years after his death. I also wish now to recall the dear memory of that Pontiff who spent himself entirely in the service of the Church. As few others, he knew how to love her, to exalt and defend her, and to explain her with a patient and wise catechesis, by expounding her intimate nature, the visible reality as well as the invisible, the external structure and the interior lymph which gives her strength and efficacy.

Now he is in the embrace of Christ, transfigured by the Resurrection: we rejoice to see him thus, while we ask the heavenly Father not to cease to let his light shine upon him, and to grant to us to follow his teachings and example which now are for us a source of edification.

* * *

1. It is important that we take the time to reread the Scripture references which the Holy Father uses. As we fix in our minds the picture upon which he focuses, the conclusion he makes becomes more apparent.

2. One of the punishments visited on those who turn away from the proper service of the Lord was exile. This was the first diaspora, scattering. But even in that first Covenant, the Lord was quick to seek out the exiles and to bring them back to Jerusalem.

3. The Pope uses an image which we might find strange. He sees Jerusalem as the home of the exiles, the Temple like a mother and the outer walls of the city the protection of the womb.

4. Turning to the Christian Covenant and especially the Gospel of St. John, the Holy Father shows us how these same themes are repeated. Now it is Jesus himself who gathers all sinners to himself to effect a perfect unity.

5. Mary is the mother of the New Jerusalem. When Jesus said to her "Woman, behold your son," he gave her as mother to all his disciples represented by St. John.

6. We pray to Mary, therefore, for the unity of all Christians that we may indeed be one People of God to the glory of the Most Holy Trinity.

7. The Church is the favorite topic of Pope John Paul II. Now as he calls our attention to Pope Paul VI, it is in terms of the efforts of that Pope to work for the good of the Church.

*August 14, 1983*
*At Castel Gandolfo*

# The Assumption of Mary

The Vigil of the Feast of the Assumption into heaven of the Blessed Virgin Mary has always been celebrated, right from the ancient times, in various forms, but always with great solemnity. In this Jubilee Year of the Redemption this occasion takes on special importance, since the glorification in body and soul of the Immaculate Mother of God, the generous partner of the Redeemer, the redemptive work of Christ the Lord reaches its first and most significant goal.

The eschatological mystery with which the historical path of Mary concludes presents, in fact, two fundamental aspects: that which refers to her person, and that which refers to Christ and to his work. From the personal aspect, the Assumption means for Mary the point of arrival of the mission which she carried out in the salvific plan of God and the crowning of all her privileges. From the Christological aspect, the glory of the Assumption and the Queenship of Mary represent the full realization of that unique decree of predestination which links the life, the privileges, the cooperation of Mary, not only to the life and the historical work of Christ, but also to his Kingship and glory as Lord.

The Assumption is the eschatological conclusion of that

From *L'Osservatore Romano* Nos. 34–35 (798) 22–29 August 1983
Title: "Pope Prays For Lebanon and Chile, Victims of Tragedy and Violence"

progressive conformation to Christ which, in the various stages of the historical path of Mary, is expressed through the inner suffering of her faith, of her hope, of her love, of her complete acceptance and availability to the salvific will of God, of her generous and responsible service to the redemptive work of her Son.

Rightly the Church recalls this Marian dogma in her faith and in her liturgy, since we celebrate in this dogma in the most significant manner the great victory of Christ over sin, over its consequences, over the corruptibility of matter and over the transience of time.

In this Jubilee Year of the Redemption, I shall have the joy of celebrating the Solemnity of the Assumption in Lourdes, where the Blessed Mother appeared eighteen times to the little Bernadette, and where I shall arrive this afternoon in pilgrimage.

I would be most grateful to you if you would accompany me with your prayers. I shall be accompanied to Lourdes by all the bitterness and anguish of the sad situations which afflict many parts of the world: I think especially of the interminable tragedy of the Lebanon and of the most recent sad events in Chile. I shall pray that it will be possible to rediscover the way of brotherhood and wisdom; I shall pray especially for the victims of violence and for their families.

At the Grotto of Massabeille, I shall remember all of you to the Blessed Mother, together with your intentions, as well as the numerous needs of the Church and of the human family.

* * *

1. The year 1983 was the 1950th anniversary of the Redemption and for that reason was celebrated as a Jubilee Year, a year of special prayer and grace. It was the redemption of Christ which earned all graces for us and the first crowning success of the redemption was the Assumption of Mary.

2. The word "eschatological" means the study of the last times, or end times. This mystery relates to Mary's "last times" when she

is taken into heaven, body, soul and spirit. It is a historical event and the crowning point of Mary's life and work.

3. Mary's Assumption is the work of Christ. What Christ has done in taking Mary, body, soul and spirit to heaven, is part of the divine plan for each of us.

4. It is easy to call Mary the Mother of Jesus. This feast of the Assumption, however, and her Queenship, emphasize the fact that we call her also, Mother of God, Mother of the Lord and Redeemer.

5. Throughout her life Mary tried to be more and more like Christ. She did this through her suffering in faith, her hope and her love. She accepted God's will and offered her self in responsible service. Now in her Assumption, she is completely conformed to Christ. The Pope calls this the "eschatological conclusion" of her effort.

6. Christ promised that we would live forever! With the celebration of the Assumption of Mary we celebrate Christ's victory over sin, death and the transience of time. We too will live forever.

7. From time to time the Holy Father adds a personal note to his Angelus message. This Sunday he invites the prayers of all to accompany him on his pilgrimage to Lourdes. He also voices his sadness at the continued violence in the world.

*August 21, 1983*
*At Castel Gandolfo*

# Mary the Image of the Church as It Will Be

Just a few days ago we celebrated the mystery of the immediate personal glorification of the Mother and Cooperator of the Redeemer immediately after the course of her earthly life. The entire Church remembered with joy this privilege of the Holy Virgin because in it she contemplates the perfect image of that final destiny of glory towards which she herself is advancing.

With the Assumption of Mary began the glorification of the whole Church of Christ which will have its completion in the final day of history. The Second Vatican Council emphasized this ecclesial reflection of the Assumption. The Immaculate Virgin of Nazareth not only constitutes the first and perfect member of the historical Church, but with her immediate glorification represents also the beginning and the perfect image of the Church of the future age. The Assumption has, both in time and in history, the value of an eschatological sign of hope for the People of God on its journey until the day of the Lord will come. By indicating her as the beginning and the image of the Church in final glory, the Council wished to tell us that with the Assumption there has already begun the Parousia of the Church, the manifestation,

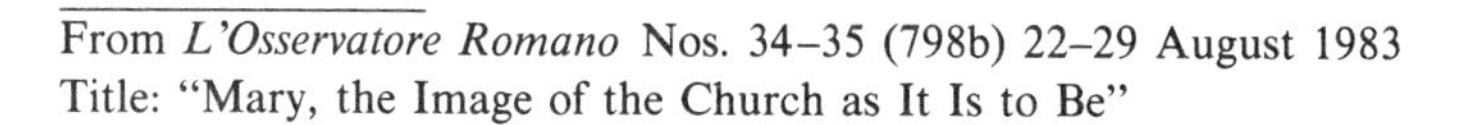
From *L'Osservatore Romano* Nos. 34–35 (798b) 22–29 August 1983
Title: "Mary, the Image of the Church as It Is to Be"

that is, of the mystical body in its fulfilled and perfect reality.

In the salvific plan of God, this event which in some respects is unique, has the finality of sign for the whole People of God: a sign of sure hope for the complete attainment of the Kingdom of God. Strengthened by this glorious sign, the Church on its historical way, awaits its own final realization, not passively or in an alienating condition, but committed to the evolution of its own historical being among the world's vicissitudes.

She knows, besides, that she can rely at every moment on the intercession of Mary assumed into the glory of heaven. The Lord, in fact, by placing her in such a condition of privilege, wishes her to be in a position to continue, in the Church and for the Church, that maternal function in favor of mankind already begun during her life on earth at the side of Christ the Redeemer. And never more than today have we experienced her as our Mother and our help.

* * *

1. The Pope reminds us that the Assumption of Mary into heaven is not simply a record of the privilege God has granted to Mary, but it is the sign and perfect image of what the Church is to be when it is in the light of glory.

2. Pope John Paul II uses two technical theological terms to express something of the depth of the mystery of the Assumption. "Eschatological" to refer to the "consideration of the last times" and "parousia" meaning "the second coming." She is the sign of hope for each of us until the Day of the Lord. What she is we shall be.

3. The Church continues to grow and develop as it makes its way through this valley of tears. In the course of this journey, Mary is the source of strength and inspiration.

4. The Assumption of Mary took place in the past. It is a sign for our future. But it is also a source of consolation to us that we can depend on her maternal help today, in our present situation.

*August 28, 1983*
*At Castel Gandolfo*

# The Joy of the Magnificat

Let us listen again today to the Virgin's hymn of praise:

> "My soul glorifies the Lord, and my spirit rejoices in God my Savior, for he has regarded the low estate of his handmaiden . . . He who is mighty has done great things for me" (Lk 1:46–49).

Already in the Old Testament, joy and thanksgiving are the usual response of all the people and of some of its members when Yahweh intervenes in their favor. And so, in the literature of the Old Testament, there flourish songs of thanksgiving both on the part of the whole assembly of Israel (Ex 15:1–18, 20–21; Is 61:10) and of individual persons (1 Sam 2:1–10; Jdg 5:1–3; Is 38:9–20; Jon 2:2–10; Dan 3:51–90; Tob 13; Jud 16:1–17 . . . cf. Lk 1:67–79 and 2:28–32). And the prayer of the psalms which served in great part for liturgical worship, taught the chosen people and each of its members to "glorify" and "thank" the Lord for the "marvelous works" done on their behalf.

Among the praying people in the New Testament, Mary, who bursts forth into her hymn of praise, that is, the "Magnificat," occupies first place.

I am pleased to quote here what my venerated predeces-

---

From *L'Osservatore Romano* No. 36 (799) 5 September 1983
Title: "Solidarity with Suffering Peoples"

sor, Paul VI wrote in the Apostolic Exhortation *Gaudete in Domino:* "Not that she is in any way spared sufferings (the Virgin Mary): she stands at the foot of the Cross, associated in an eminent way with the sacrifice of the innocent Servant. But she is also open in an unlimited degree to the joy of the Resurrection; and she is also taken up, body and soul, into the glory of heaven . . . she is the perfect model of the Church both on earth and in glory. With Christ she sums up in herself all joys: she lives the perfect joy promised to the Church: '*Mater plena sanctae laetitiae.*' And it is with good reason that her children on earth, turning to her who is the mother of hope and of grace, invoke her as the cause of their joy."

Dear brothers and sisters, the contemplation of the Most Blessed Virgin, then, rejuvenates our joy and makes it active, as Paul VI exhorted in the above-mentioned document: "Without departing from a realistic viewpoint, let Christian communities become centers of optimism, where all the members resolutely endeavour to perceive the positive aspect of people and events . . . The attainment of such an outlook is not just a matter of psychology. It is also a fruit of the Holy Spirit . . . This positive outlook . . . finds in Christians a privileged place of replenishment: the celebration of the Paschal Mystery of Jesus . . . the sign and source of Christian joy, the preparation for the eternal feast" (Acta Sancta Sede, p. 321, 322).

* * *

1. When the Lord intervenes in our lives, our response is one of joy. This was the case with Moses, Isaiah, Tobias and others in the Old Testament.

2. In the New Testament, the response to the work of God is the same: joy. The most important example of this is Mary as she sings her Magnificat.

3. As he quotes Pope Paul VI, the Holy Father reminds us of the sufferings of Mary standing at the foot of the Cross and from her being so closely united with the sacrifice of Jesus. At the same

time, she rejoices with Jesus in the unlimited joy of the Resurrection and her Assumption into heaven.

4. Mary lives in the perfect joy which is promised to the Church. She is "Mother who is filled with holy joy" and the cause of our joy.

5. He tells us that while we are to keep our feet on the ground we must cultivate a positive outlook. Christian joy does not come from some psychological trick but from the celebration of the Pascal Mystery of Jesus.

*September 4, 1983*
*At Castel Gandolfo*

# Mary, Seat of Wisdom

We invoke the Holy Virgin as the "Seat of Wisdom." But, what is Wisdom? Or, better, who is Wisdom?

In some texts of the Old Testament, developed especially after the Babylonian exile, Wisdom was identified with the Law of Moses (Deut 4:6; Sir 24:1–25; Bar 3:12,4:1 . . .), rather than with the complex of the Sacred Scriptures (Sir, prologue 1–3;6–14). In those venerable books is documented the history of the Lord with his people and, therefore, manifested in them is God's Wisdom, that is, his plan, his thought, regarding not only Israel, but the whole of humanity and all creation (Sir 42:15;50:24; Wis 8:8;9:9–18;10:1–19,22 . . . ).

As a consequence, the wise man is the one who reads, studies the Sacred Books and guards the Torah in his heart in order to glean from it lessons for life (Ps 107:1–42; Sir 50:27–28 . . . ).

This loving attention to sacred history becomes more intense during the days of suffering (Jud 8:25–29 . . . ), that is, when God's behaviour seems to be enigmatic (Sir 4:17–18): "For deeper than the sea are her thoughts; her counsels, than the great abyss" (Sir 24:27).

The pious Israelite, made wise by the teaching of the

From *L'Osservatore Romano* No. 37 (800) 12 September 1983
Title: "Mary Seat of Wisdom"

Scriptures, looks at men and the world with God's point of view. Rather, living in this way, he makes very special bonds with him: he becomes a son (Sir 15:2), a brother (Prv 7:4), a friend (Wis 8:18), and a spouse of Wisdom (Wis 8:2, 9:16; Sir 15:2).

The message of the New Testament teaches that Christ is the "Wisdom of God" (1 Cor 1:24). In his person, in his words and in his acts, the Father reveals in a definite way what his plan of salvation is (cf.Lk 7:29,30,35). It is a plan difficult to understand since it passes through the scandal of suffering and the Cross (1 Cor 1:25).

Mary, Most Holy is the "Seat of Wisdom" since she welcomed Jesus, Wisdom incarnate, into her heart and into her womb. With the "fiat" of the Annunciation, she agreed to serve the divine will, and Wisdom made his dwelling in her bosom, making her an exemplary disciple. The Virgin was blessed not so much for having nursed the Son of God but rather for having nourished herself with the health-giving milk of the word of God (cf. Lk 11:27–28).

In imitation of Mary, the heart of every believer is transformed into a dwelling place of Christ-Wisdom. Similar to what happened between the true Israelite and Wisdom, a mysterious form of Spiritual relationship is also established between us and the Lord. Jesus himself says so: "Whoever does the will of my heavenly Father is brother and sister and mother to me" (Mt 12:50; cf. Mk 3:53; Lk 8:21).

May Mary guide us and help us to live our relations with Jesus the Redeemer in this way.

* * *

1. Here the Holy Father becomes our teacher in a special way as he reflects the findings of current Scripture scholarship about the dating of the various Books of the Bible. He shows how the different dates of composition provide nuances which in turn lead to important insights into the meaning of the Scriptures.

2. "Wisdom" he tells us, is not a thing, it is a person. It is the person who reads, studies and guards the Scriptures within his heart and so learns how to live.

3. Wisdom allows one to look at the world from God's perspective. Such a one is son, brother, friend and spouse.

4. St. Paul tells us that "Christ is the wisdom of God." In him, in his life, his word, his Passion, Death and Resurrection, God's plan is revealed.

5. As we reflect on all this, we can see how the words of Jesus about his mother—that she will be more blessed because she has heard his word and kept it—are the result of Jesus' own special knowledge of the Scriptures. Mary, therefore, is the Seat of Wisdom.

*September 11, 1983*
*In Vienna*

# The Angelus, a Sign of Christian Hope

On September 11, 1983, the Pope was on pilgrimage in Austria. He introduced the Angelus with the following words:

Dear Brothers and Sisters,

At the end of this solemn Mass let us together recite the midday Marian prayer. It reminds us every day how our Christian hope had its origin in the threefold event: the angel of the Lord brings Mary the message. Mary says: "Let it be done to me as you have said"—and the Word becomes one of us. We all wish to open ourselves once again to the message that God has sent to us so that his word may become flesh also in our lives.

* * *

1. While the Holy Father is on a pastoral visit to Austria, he invites all who are present with him to pray the Angelus, a sign of the origin of our Christian hope.

2. The sign of our Christian hope comes to us in a drama of three scenes. First, the Lord God shows his loving concern for the world by sending his angel with the joyful message: "Hail Mary, full of grace, the Lord is with you."

---

From *L'Osservatore Romano* No.38 (801) 19 September 1983
Title: "The Angelus a Sign of Christian Hope"

3. The second scene emphasizes the drama in which the Lord and all creation wait for Mary's answer. "Be it done unto me according to your will." Fiat.

4. The Word was made flesh and dwelt among us. This is the third and continuing scene of the divine drama. God becomes man in Jesus to redeem the world. The Incarnation!

5. The Incarnation! The wonder of it. Is there any question then, that the Holy Father invites us to recall the origin of our Christian hope?

6. As we pray we must open ourselves so that each day we allow the Word of God to become flesh in our lives once again.

*September 18, 1983*

# Mary, Mother of Consolation

"Consoler of the Afflicted": here is another dimension of Mary's motherly presence in the Church and in the world.

Consolation, according to the teachings of the Old Testament, has its origin in God, who pours it out upon all his creatures.

When the Lord leads the exiles back to Palestine, he will make Jerusalem the sanctuary of his consolation. In the heart of the Holy City all the people will be gathered and each one will be able to experience God's tenderness.

In this regard the divine message, expressed by the Prophet Isaiah, poetically uses feminine images. Jerusalem is compared to a mother who nurses her infants and surrounds them with loving care: "Oh, that you may suck fully of the milk of her comfort, that you may nurse with delight at her abundant breasts! . . . As nurslings you shall be carried in her arms, and fondled in her lap" (Is 66:11,13).

Passing on then to its application, this symbolic language is interpreted in the following words: "As a mother comforts her son, so will I comfort you; in Jerusalem you shall find your comfort" (Is 66:13).

And the Messiah, in the expectation of the Chosen People, was to be "the consolation of Israel" (Lk 2:26).

---

From *L'Osservatore Romano* No.39 (802), 26 September 1983
Title: "Mary, Mother of Consolation"

With Christ's redemptive work a new Jerusalem is born, that is, the Church. In this family God's love, becoming tangible in the heart of Christ, consoles, fondling in his lap, as it were, every person coming into this world.

And speaking of the Church, the discourse uniquely touches the Holy Virgin, who is the Mother of the Church (Jn 19:25–27) and the perfect model of the Lord's disciples (Second Vatican Council, *Sacrosanctum Concilium,* 103; Paul VI *Marialis Cultus,* 37). With the same overflowing charity with which she takes care of the brethren of his Son, God, "rich in mercy" (Eph 2:4), gives us, so to speak, the motherly outpouring of his consolation.

As I wrote in the encyclical *Dives in Misericordia:* "It was precisely this 'merciful love,' which is manifested above all in contact with moral and physical evil, that the heart of her who was the Mother of the Crucified and Risen One shared in singularly and exceptionally—that Mary shared in. In her and though her, this love continues to be revealed in the history of the Church and of humanity" (*Acta Sancta Sede* 72, 1980, p.1209).

Bothers and sisters, you realize this already! In order worthily to venerate the Holy Virgin as the "Mother of Consolation" we must appear before the world as crystal-clear signs of God's consolation (cf. 2 Cor 1:3–7). It must not escape anyone how in our Christian communities human dignity is promoted, protected and redeemed in the event it has been degraded. In the words of the Apostle, let our commitment be to rejoice with those who rejoice and to weep with those who weep (Rom 12:15).

For this task, may Mary still be our inspiring model: she who was present at the happiness of the marriage of Cana (Jn 2:1) and at the tragedy of Calvary (Jn 19:25).

* * *

1. As we read the Hebrew Scriptures there is one attribute of the Lord which we sometimes miss. It is his tenderness. When the

exiles return to Palestine, the Lord surrounded them with his tenderness.

2. To emphasize this tenderness even more, the poetic images which the Scriptures use are feminine and maternal. It is as though the Lord were fondling and suckling these returning infants. Is the Pope trying to say: God is our mother!

3. With Christ, the New Jerusalem is the Church. God is likewise the consolation of these new children, and the sign of his love is the heart of Christ.

4. Mary was close to the suffering Christ on Calvary and the risen Christ of Easter. Because of this closeness with the Savior, Mary is the one through whom God reveals his merciful love.

5. If we are to be of any comfort to the world in which we live, and if we are to offer proper veneration to Mary, we ourselves must show that we have received the consolation which the Lord has given. We are to be signs of this consolation to the world.

6. Finally, drawing on the point which he had made just before, the Pope reminds us that the joy of Cana and the pain of Calvary make Mary our model to this day.

*September 25, 1983*

# Mary Teaches Us the True Meaning of Poverty

"He has looked upon his servant in her lowliness . . . He has deposed the mighty from their thrones and raised the lowly to high places" (Lk 1:48,52). With these words the Virgin exalts divine wisdom, who is pleased with the lowly and confounds those who trust only in their own certainty.

"Poverty" is a virtue slowly acquired by the spirituality of the Old Testament. As a result of the Babylonian Exile, a more internalized significance of this virtue develops. That is to say: the "poor" is the one who wholeheartedly complies with the Lord, obeying his will as concretely expressed in the Law of Moses (cf. Zeph 3:12–13; Is 66:2; Jdt 9:11,14).

Poverty conceived in this way was not reduced to an empty privacy capable of shirking duties of social justice. On the contrary, the observance of the Law of Moses produced visible results of fraternity. In fact, it was a pressing obligation to help the needy, the widow, the orphan, the slave, the stranger; it also provided for the settling of debts on the occasion of the sabbatical jubilee year.

Mary, the Second Vatican Council writes, "stands out among the poor and humble of the Lord, who confidently await and receive salvation from him" (*Lumen Gentium,* 55).

---

From *L'Osservatore Romano* No.40 (803), 3 October 1983
Title: "Poverty Cares for the Needs of Others"

Mary's poverty is the sublimation of the poverty lived by so many of the just in the Old Testament. The Annunciation is the emblematic proof of the Virgin as a creature "poor in spirit," who with her "fiat" opens herself in perfect docility to God's will (Lk 1:49,52,54).

Right up to the day of her passing to heavenly glory, Mary's poverty will consist in her generous dedication to the person and the work of her Son. And always in the lights and the shadows of faith! (cf. Lk 2:34; 35,48–50; Acts 1:14; 4:23–30; 8:1–3; 12:1; 28:22).

For us too, disciples of the Lord, poverty of spirit amounts to unconditional obedience to his Gospel. It is an education of the heart, which Paul asks for in these words: "Your attitude must be that of Christ" (Phil 2:5; cf. Mt 11:28–29; Jas 1:21).

The same social question, understood as just distribution of goods, both economic and moral, depends as much as ever on the same kind of poverty. Sincere compliance with Christ's word does not tolerate the shame of injustice, of oppression. The early community of Jerusalem, to which Mary belonged (Acts 1:14), "devoted themselves to the Apostles' instruction and the communal life, to the breaking of bread and the prayers" (Acts 2:42), and as a result of this evangelical fervor, there was no one in need among them (Acts 2:44–45; 4:32,34–35; cf. Dt 15:4 and 2 Cor 8:13).

May Christ stir up Mary's poverty in us! Then the power of his Spirit will give free rein to the "great things" of the Redemption. Then we will be blessed, because ours is the Kingdom of Heaven (cf. Mt 5:3).

* * *

1. When the chosen people returned from exile, they were poor. They had nothing. They had to rely entirely on the Lord. They learned a new kind of poverty, poverty of spirit.

2. The Law of Moses required that even the poor, those without material resources, still had social responsibilities. They had to care

for the needs of the disadvantaged, the widow, orphan, slave and stranger. Social obligations became religious obligations as well.

3. Mary depended entirely on the Lord. She is the perfect example of docility to the will of God. By her "fiat" she raised the poverty of the Old Testament to new heights.

4. We do not know just when Mary died. The Pope assumes that it was sometime after the death of Jesus so that Mary shared the hardships of persecution with the rest of the early Christian community. She shared in them with the same total, generous dedication which marked her whole life.

5. Today we are called on to have the same unconditional obedience to the Gospel. Just as in the early Christian community, Mary is our model of evangelical fervor, and neither can we tolerate injustice or oppression in our day.

6. As the Lord had done "great things" to Mary so may we expect great things in us if we imitate her poverty of spirit.

*October 2, 1983*

# The Rosary, The Heart of the Christian Message

During the month of October, traditionally consecrated to the Holy Rosary, I wish to dedicate the Angelus thought to this prayer that is so dear to the heart of Catholics, so loved by me, and so recommended by the Popes who have preceded me.

In this extraordinary Holy Year of the Redemption, the Rosary too acquires new perspectives and is laden with greater and vaster intentions than in the past. Today it is not a matter of asking for great victories, as at Lepanto and Vienna, but rather of asking Mary to make us brave soldiers against the spirit of error and evil, with the arms of the Gospel, which are the Cross and the Word of God.

The Rosary is a prayer of man for man: it is the prayer of human solidarity, a collegial prayer of the redeemed, which reflects the spirit and the intentions of the first redeemed, Mary, Mother and image of the Church: a prayer for all men and women of the world and of history, living or deceased, called to be, with us, the Body of Christ and to become with him co-heirs of the Father's glory.

Considering the spiritual orientations suggested by the Rosary, a simple evangelical prayer (cf. *Marialis Cultus,* 46), we

From *L'Osservatore Romano* No. 41 (804), 10 October 1983
Title: "Armed with the Cross and Word of God"

discover the intentions that St. Cyprian noted in the Our Father. He wrote: "The Lord, Master of peace and unity, did not want us to pray individually and by ourselves. Indeed, we do not say 'My Father, who are in heaven' nor 'Give me this day my daily bread.' Our prayer is for everybody; so much so that when we pray, we do so not just for one, but for all people, because with all people we are just one" (*De dominica oratione,* 8).

The Rosary is addressed with perseverance to her who is the greatest expression of mankind at prayer, the model of the Church praying and asking, in Christ, for the Father's mercy. As Christ is "forever living to make intercession for us" (cf. Heb 7:25), so Mary continues in heaven her mission as Mother and makes herself the voice of every man, until the eternal fulfillment of all the elect (cf. *Lumen Gentium,* 62). Praying to her, we ask her to assist us throughout our whole present life and above all at that moment that will be decisive for our eternal destiny, the "hour of our death." The Rosary is the prayer that points to the perspective of the Kingdom of God and disposes man to receive the fruits of the Redemption.

* * *

1. The Holy Father tells us of his own devotion to the Rosary, a devotion which he shares with all Catholics and which had been so praised and recommended by the Popes in the past.

2. Today, our prayers are not to accompany armies in the field, but to strengthen ourselves for the battle with the principalities and powers, the spirit of evil and error. This strength will come from the Cross and the Scriptures.

3. The Rosary is a prayer of human solidarity. It passes bonds of culture and language. When we pray the Rosary, we are one with one another and one with Mary. We reflect her spirit and her intention to do the work of Christ.

4. In this, Mary is the Mother, the image and example of the Church praying with everyone, living and dead in the one Body of Christ. It is in praying that we become, with Christ, coheirs of the Father's glory.

5. One thought deserves special mention. The Rosary is a simple evangelical prayer. The images and the words are simply the words we take from the Gospel.

6. The Holy Father turns to St. Cyprian who in the third century reminded us that when we pray, we do not pray alone. We pray to "Our" Father and with all the people, we are one.

7. Quoting from the Second Vatican Council, the Holy Father reminds us that Mary continues in heaven her mission to be the voice of every person until the fullness of time. In this she is like Christ, always making intercession for us.

8. Mary, pray for us now and at the hour of our death.

*October 9, 1983*

# The Rosary Reflects the Redemption

Among the many aspects that Popes, saints and scholars have noted in the Rosary, one is duly recalled in this Jubilee Year. The Holy Rosary is a continued remembrance of the Redemption in its outstanding stages: the Incarnation of the Word, his passion and death for us, the Pasch that he inaugurated and that will find its eternal fulfillment in heaven.

Indeed, while considering the contemplative elements of the Rosary, that is, the mysteries around which the vocal prayer unfolds, we can better understand why this crown of "Ave's" has been called the "Virgin's Psalter." As the Psalms reminded Israel of the marvels of the Exodus and of the salvation wrought by God, and constantly recalled the people to fidelity to the pact of Sinai, so the Rosary continually reminds the New Covenant people of the wonders of mercy and power that God has unfolded in Christ on behalf of man, and recalls them to fidelity with regard to their baptismal commitments. We are his people, he is our God.

But this remembrance of God's wonders and this constant recall to fidelity passes in a certain way through Mary, the faithful Virgin. The succession of "Ave's" helps us to penetrate, from time to time, ever more deeply into the greatest

---

From *L'Osservatore Romano* No. 42 (805) 17 October 1983
Title: "The Rosary Recalls the Redemption in its Outstanding Stages"

mystery of the Incarnate Word and Savior (cf. *Lumen Gentium,* 65), "with the heart of the one who was closest to the Lord" (*Marialis Cultus,* 47). Because Mary too, as Daughter of Sion and heiress of the wisdom spirituality of Israel, sang the wonders of the Exodus. But as the first and most perfect disciple of Christ, she anticipated and lived the Pasch of the New Covenant, preserving in her heart and meditating on every word and every act of her Son, associating herself with him in unconditional fidelity, pointing out to everyone the path of the new pact: "Do whatever he tells you" (Jn 2:5). Glorified today in heaven, she shows completed in herself the new people's itinerary towards the Promised Land.

May the Rosary therefore immerse us in the mysteries of Christ, and on the face of his Mother, may every Christian and the whole Church see the model of how to welcome, preserve and live God's every word and event, on the ongoing road of salvation of the world.

* * *

1. The "Jubilee Year" is the celebration of the 1950th anniversary of the death and resurrection of Christ. The jubilee is a time of special prayer and indulgence.

2. The mysteries of the Rosary focus on the central messages of Christianity: the death and resurrection of Jesus for the salvation of the world, his Pasch.

3. The Book of Psalms in the Hebrew Scriptures is called "the Psalter." It is a collection of 150 songs of praise recalling the goodness of the Lord God in saving his people. As they were reminded of God's goodness, the people were recalled to fidelity to God's promises.

4. The Rosary, the "Virgin's Psalter," likewise reminds us continually of the wonders of the mercy and power of the Lord given to his people in the New Covenant. It recalls us to fidelity to the commitment we made in our Baptism.

5. Time and again the Holy Father reminds us that Mary was a Jew and so was very familiar with the Hebrew Scriptures. She gave thanks to the Lord for the deliverance of Exodus. Now she

is the first and most perfect disciple of Christ. She is also first in leading us to give thanks for our deliverance on Calvary.

6. Mary instructs us as well; her directions to the servants at Cana are her directions to us as well. Her words: "Do whatever he tells you," give direction to our lives.

7. Before all else, Mary is an example. We see in her the way that we must preserve and live God's every Word on our way to salvation.

*October 16, 1983*

# The Holy Father Renews the Appeal Made at Fatima; "Deliver Us from War and From Sins Against Life"

## "We have recourse to your protection, holy Mother of God."

**O** mother of individuals and peoples, you who "know all their sufferings and their hopes," you who have a mother's awareness of all the struggles between good and evil, between light and darkness, which afflict the modern world, accept the cry which we, as though moved by the Holy Spirit, address directly to your Heart. Embrace, with the love of the Mother and Handmaid, this human world of ours, which we entrust and consecrate to you, for we are full of disquiet for the earthly and eternal destiny of individuals and peoples.

In a special way we entrust and consecrate to you those individuals and nations which particularly need to be entrusted and consecrated.

"We have recourse to your protection, holy Mother of

---

From *L'Osservatore Romano* No. 43 (806) 24 October 1983
Title: "The Holy Father Renews the Appeal Made at Fatima: 'Deliver us from War and from Sins Against Life' "

God: reject not the prayers we send up to you in our necessities."

Reject them not!

Accept our humble trust—and our act of entrusting!

"For God so loved the world that he gave his only Son, that whoever believes in him should not perish but have eternal life" (Jn 3:16).

It was precisely by reason of this love that the Son of God consecrated himself for all mankind: "And for their sake I consecrate myself, that they also may be consecrated in truth" (Jn 17:19).

By reason of that consecration the disciples of all ages are called to spend themselves for the salvation of the world, and to supplement Christ's afflictions for the sake of his body, that is the Church (cf. 2 Cor 12:15; Col 1:24).

Before you, Mother of Christ, before your Immaculate Heart, I today, together with the whole Church, unite myself with our Redeemer in this his consecration for the world and for people which only in his divine Heart has the power to obtain pardon and to secure reparation.

The power of this consecration lasts for all time and embraces all individuals, peoples and nations. It overcomes every evil that the spirit of darkness is able to awaken, and has in fact awakened in our times, in the heart of man and in his history.

The Church, the Mystical Body of Christ, unites herself, through the service of Peter's successor, to this consecration by our Redeemer.

Oh, how deeply we feel the need for consecration on the part of humanity and of the world—our modern world—in union with Christ himself! The redeeming work of Christ, in fact, must be shared in by the world by means of the Church.

Oh, how pained we are by all the things in the Church and in each one of us that are opposed to holiness and consecration! How pained we are that the invitation to repentance, to conversion, to prayer, has not met with the acceptance that it should have received!

How pained we are that many share so coldly in Christ's work of Redemption! That "what is lacking in Christ's afflictions" is so insufficiently completed in our flesh.

And so, blessed be all those souls that obey the call of eternal Love! Blessed be all those who, day after day, with undiminished generosity accept your invitation, O Mother, to do what your Jesus tells them and give the Church and the world a serene testimony of lives inspired by the Gospel.

Above all, blessed be you, the Handmaid of the Lord, who in the fullest way obeys the divine call!

Hail to you, who are "wholly united" to the redeeming consecration of your Son!

Mother of the Church! Enlighten the People of God along the paths of faith, of hope and love! Help us to live with the whole truth of consecration of Christ for the entire human family of the modern world.

In entrusting to you, O Mother, the world, all individuals and peoples, we also entrust to you the consecration itself, for the world's sake, placing it in your motherly Heart.

Oh, Immaculate Heart! Help us to conquer the menace of evil, which so easily takes root in the hearts of the people of today, and whose immeasurable effects already weigh down upon our modern world and seem to block the paths towards the future!

From famine and war, deliver us.

From nuclear war, from incalculable self-destruction, from every kind of war, deliver us.

From sins against the life of man from its very beginning, deliver us.

From hatred and from the demeaning of the dignity of the children of God, deliver us.

From every kind of injustice in the life of society, both national and international, deliver us.

From readiness to trample on the commandments of God, deliver us.

From sins against the Holy Spirit, deliver us, deliver us.

Accept, O Mother of Christ, this cry laden with the sufferings of all individual human beings, laden with the sufferings of whole societies.

Let there be revealed once more in the history of the world the infinite power of merciful Love. May it put a stop to evil. May it transform consciences. May your Immaculate Heart reveal for all the light of hope! Amen.

* * *

1. At Fatima, Our Lady asked that the Holy Father and all the bishops consecrate the world to Mary. Pope John Paul II made this consecration at Fatima in 1982 and now, in union with bishops from throughout the world, he makes this consecration again.

2. The consecration is clothed in terms of our needs and our hopes. Yet, as we listen to them, we hear the echoes of the themes found in the Angelus Messages which he has been delivering each Sunday of this year.

3. This prayer of the Holy Father and our prayer as well, is built upon the strong foundations of a clear understanding and appreciation of Mary's place in the whole mystery of salvation. That is, this prayer is built on the foundation which the Holy Father is supplying with the other messages of this series.

*October 23, 1983*
*Mission Sunday*

# The Joyful Mysteries of the Rosary

The holy Rosary is a Christian, evangelical and ecclesial prayer, but it is also a prayer that elevates the sentiments and affections of man.

In the joyful mysteries, on which we pause briefly today, we see some of all this: the joy of the family, of motherhood, of relatives, of friendship, of mutual help. These joys, which sin has not totally destroyed, Christ has assumed in himself and sanctified by his birth.

He did this through Mary. And so it is through her that we, even today, can gather and make our own the joys of man, in themselves humble and simple, but which in Mary and in Jesus become great and holy.

In Mary, virginally betrothed to Joseph and divinely fruitful, there is the joy of the chaste love of spouses and of motherhood welcomed and cared for as a gift from God. In Mary, who caringly goes to visit Elizabeth, there is the joy of serving one's brothers and sisters by bringing them God's presence. In Mary, who presents to the shepherds and the Magi the Expected One of Israel, there is the spontaneous and trusting sharing that is typical of friendship. In Mary, who offers her Son in the Temple to the heavenly Father,

---

From *L'Osservatore Romano* No. 44 (807) 31 Oct. 1983
Title: "In Jesus and Mary Our Joys Become Great and Holy"

there is the joy drenched with anxiety, typical of parents and teachers for their children or pupils. In Mary, who after three days of worried searching finds Jesus, there is the joy that her child belongs to God before belonging to her.

Today the Church is observing World Mission Day. On the occasion of this observance, this morning I celebrated the Eucharist in the Basilica of St. Paul Outside the Walls, where I presented crucifixes to a group of priests, religious and lay persons who are leaving for the missions.

"The harvest is good, but the laborers are scarce" (Mt 9:37). Brothers and sisters, we must reinforce our concern for the missionary problem with a greater support, both spiritual and material, for the works of the missions: cultural and welfare institutions, schools, hospitals, social works which constitute the "signs of credibility" and at the same time the very witness of an effective missionary activity.

* * *

1. The Rosary is a Christian prayer. It focuses on the central mystery of Christianity, the salvation of the world by Christ.

2. It is an evangelic prayer. The prayers which are said and the mysteries which are contemplated are taken from the Gospels and reflect its message of "good news."

3. The Rosary is the prayer of the Church and the mostly widely spread devotion to Mary. The People of God, the Church has made it its own prayer.

4. What has made the Rosary as popular as it is? It reflects our fundamental human experiences and sentiments and elevates them to instruments of prayer and contemplation.

5. Mary and Joseph exhibit the joy of chaste love and family life. The visit to Elizabeth reflects the joy of serving and of bringing the gift of Christ to others. Offering the Christ child to the shepherds and to the Magi shows them joy of trusting friendship.

6. The scene in the Temple reflects the joy of anticipation even if it is mixed with anxiety. This meditation also reminds us of the joy found in the realization of God being first in our lives.

7. The Rosary is not just about past mysteries but about present joys and experiences which are raised to the Lord in prayer.

8. The Holy Father adds to his Marian message a message about the missions of the Church and how they deserve our support.

*October 30, 1983*

# The Sorrowful Mysteries of the Rosary

On this last Sunday of October, we pause to reflect again on the Rosary.

In the sorrowful mysteries we contemplate in Christ all the sorrows of man: in Christ in agony, betrayed, abandoned, captured, imprisoned; in Christ unjustly tried and subjected to scourging; in Christ misunderstood and ridiculed in his mission; in Christ condemned with complicity of the political power; in Christ led publicly to torture and sentenced to the most shameful death: in him, the Man of Sorrows foretold by Isaiah, every human sorrow is taken up and sanctified.

Servant of the Father, First-born among many brothers, Head of mankind, he transforms man's suffering into an oblation pleasing to God in a redeeming sacrifice. It is he, the Lamb of God who takes away the sin of the world, the faithful Witness, who sums up in himself and makes meritorious every martyrdom.

On his sorrowful way and on Golgotha there is his Mother, the first martyr. And with the heart of his Mother, to whom he bequeathed from the cross every disciple and every person, we contemplate with emotion the sufferings of Christ, learning from him obedience to death, even to the

---

From *L'Osservatore Romano* No. 45 (808) 7 November 1983
Title: "Pope Reflects on Sorrowful Mysteries"

death on a cross; learning from her to accept every man as a brother, in order to stand with her at the innumerable crosses on which the Lord of glory is still unjustly nailed, not in his glorious body, but in the suffering members of his Mystical Body.

* * *

1. In his recollection on the sorrowful mysteries of the Rosary, the Holy Father points out that Jesus suffered agony, betrayal, abandonment, imprisonment, unjust trials and humiliations. He had to suffer all these human trials because of the betrayal by public officials. Finally, he was sentenced to a shameful death. Every conceivable human sorrow may be seen in the suffering of Jesus during his passion and death.

2. Isaiah the Prophet announced the "Man of Sorrows." (Is 53:3) That man is Jesus.

3. Jesus who was "Servant of the Father" (Act 3:13), did not suffer just for the sake of suffering. His sufferings were a redeeming sacrifice which takes away the sins of the world. His sacrifice validates every sacrifice.

4. The Holy Father tells us that the very best way to contemplate the sorrows of Jesus is through the heart of his Mother Mary. She is our mother as well.

5. Today Jesus is being crucified again. Now it is in the suffering members of his Mystical Body who are being nailed unjustly to innumerable crosses.

*November 1, 1983*

# Mary is the Firstborn and Mother of the Church of the Saints

"Who are these people all dressed in white, and where have they come from?" (Rev 7:13).

Who are the Saints?

The saints are those who have put on the white clothing of the "new Man" (Col 3:10), bringing their baptismal grace to its full development. They are sharers and witnesses of the holy God, the "hidden God" (Is 45:15). Thanks to them, he is revealed, made visible and present among us. The "Holy One of God" is, obviously, Christ Jesus, the incarnation and supreme revelation of God and his sanctity. "You alone are the Holy One, you alone are the Lord, you alone are the Most High, Jesus Christ."

Constituted "Lord" in his glorious resurrection, Jesus, through the Holy Spirit, communicates his sanctity to all believers. They, in the sacraments worthily received, receive new life in Christ Jesus. They are therefore called holy, and they really are.

Where have they come from?

Let us listen to the description from the Book of Revelation: "I heard the number of those who were so marked—one hundred and forty-four thousand from every tribe of Israel . . .

---

From *L'Osservatore Romano* No. 45 (808a) 7 November 1983
Title: "Mary is the Firstborn and Mother of the Church of the Saints"

After this I saw before me a huge crowd which no one could count from every nation and race, people and tongue. . . .
These are the ones who have survived the great period of trial; they have washed their robes and made them white in the blood of the Lamb" (Rev. 7:4,9,14).

The saints are the People of God redeemed by the blood of the Lord: an immense multitude coming from the tribes of Israel and from all the peoples. Together they constitute the "true Israel," the community of the saved, the Church of God, the descendants of Abraham in whom all the nations are blessed. In the midst of this most noble, endless line, alongside Christ there is Mary, whom we invoke as the "Queen of All Saints." She, who "stands out among the poor and humble of the Lord" (*Lumen Gentium,* 55), ideally embodies and brings to completion the sanctity of the People of God. Mary is the first born and Mother of the Church of the saints: of all those who, born of the Spirit and living in Christ, are children of the Father.

The Spirit of the living God who preserved her beforehand and formed a new creature, who decisively intervened in her life by consecrating her the servant and Mother of the Lord, has in the end transfigured her existence, conforming her to the image of Christ in glory.

She lives now with the Lord, in the heavenly Jerusalem, and she celebrates with St. Joseph and all the saints the eternal liturgy of the redeemed. She intercedes for us with the Lord, until the eternal crowning of the number of the elect. With the People of God we invoke her: "Queen of All Saints, pray for us!"

* * *

1. Who are the saints? The saints are they who have been born again and who have brought their baptismal promises to fulfillment.

2. The saints are like sacraments. They reveal and make God visible and present among us.

3. Saints are saints because Christ communicates to them his own holiness. They are holy because they have received this new life in Christ.

4. The Saints are saints because they have been redeemed by the Blood of the Lord. First among all the saints: Mary. Mary is the firstborn. Mary is the Mother of the Church and so mother of the saints.

5. It was the Lord who had preserved and transformed Mary into the perfect image of her Son. First He established her as his servant.

6. Mary and her blessed spouse Joseph live with the Lord and continue to intercede for us until the completion of the number of the elect.

7. Queen of All Saints, pray for us.

*November 6, 1983*

# The Glorious Mysteries of the Rosary

In the glorious mysteries of the Holy Rosary we relive the Christian's hopes: the hopes for eternal life, which engage God's omnipotence, and the expectations of the present time, which engage men's collaboration with God.

In Christ who rises, the whole world rises, and there begin the new heavens and the new earth, which will find their completion on his glorious return, when "there shall be no more death or mourning, crying out or pain, for the former world has passed away" (Rev 21:4).

In him who ascends into heaven, human nature is exalted, placed at the right hand of God, and there is given to the disciples the task of evangelizing the world. Besides, in ascending to heaven, Christ has not disappeared from the earth: He is hidden in the countenance of every person, especially in the most unhappy: the poor, the sick, those discriminated against, the persecuted . . .

Pouring forth the Holy Spirit on Pentecost, he gave the disciples the power to love and to spread the truth, he asked them to share in building a world worthy of redeemed man, and he gave them the power to sanctify all things in obedience to the will of the heavenly Father. In this way he rekin-

From *L'Osservatore Romano* No.46 (809) 14 November 1983
Title: "The Rosary Expresses Mankind's Hopes"

dled, in the soul of whoever gives, the joy of giving; and, in the heart of whoever is unhappy, the certainty that he is loved.

In the glory of the Virgin, assumed and first redeemed, we contemplate among other things the true sublimation of blood ties and family affections: Christ in fact glorified Mary not only because she is immaculate and the ark of the Divine Presence, but also in order to honor his Mother as a son: the holy bonds of earth are not broken in heaven. And what is more, in the solicitude of the Virgin Mary, assumed in order to become our advocate and protectress, the type of the Church Triumphant, we perceive the very model inspiring the attentive love of our dear departed for us, a love that is not broken by death but is made powerful in God's light.

Finally, in looking at Mary glorified by all creatures we celebrate the eschatological mystery of a humanity recomposed in Christ in perfect unity, with no more divisions, no rivalries, except to anticipate one another in love. Because God is love.

In the mysteries of the Holy Rosary we therefore contemplate and relive the joys, sorrows and glories of Christ and his holy Mother, which become the joys, sorrows and hopes of man.

* * *

1. The Pope had interrupted his October series on the Rosary with his trip to Fatima. Here he takes up his reflections on the Rosary with a meditation on the glorious mysteries and relates them to our personal hopes and expectations.

2. Hope, he tells us, is of two kinds. The first depends entirely on God and his power. This is the hope of everlasting life. The second depends on our cooperation with God. This pertains to our expectations in this life.

3. Our faith makes us one with Christ. With him we died on the Cross and with him we too hope to rise from the dead. Yet he is with us even as we await his return in glory.

4. Christ is not invisible. We can see him in those who are unhappy, the poor, the sick, those who are discriminated against or persecuted.

5. When Christ sent the Holy Spirit upon his disciples, he gave the responsibility of building a world worthy of the redeemed. The spiritual message has a social dimension. Giving to others is an obligation and a joy.

6. We can be certain of this, God loves us. This transforms sadness into joy.

7. Even in heaven, the bonds of family and affection are not broken. Jesus crowns his mother Queen not just because of her privileges, but just because she is his mother.

8. The Holy Father calls Mary a "type" of the Church Triumphant. That is as Mary herself intercedes for us, so too do all our relatives and friends, now part of the Church Triumphant, continue their intercession for us.

9. The Pope uses the technical term "eschatology"—the study of the final things—to remind us that in heaven there will be only one rivalry, that of trying to anticipate each other in love (Rom 12:10).

*November 13, 1983*

# At Prayer with Mary, the Mother of Jesus

The Church is above all a praying community. The People of God have been liberated to celebrate the worship of the Lord. The whole life of the redeemed must be an act of worship, a liturgy of praise, a sacrifice pleasing to God. The transformation of our life and of the world into a sacrifice of praise is not our work, but the Lord's. Uniting ourselves with Christ the Priest, with his sacrifice and his prayer, we along with the whole universe, become an offering to the Lord.

Believers are essentially a liturgical community: in Church, in homes, in life, they exercise the priestly office. The Acts of the Apostles in presenting the basic outlines of the early Church, stress the importance that "prayer" has in it: "They devoted themselves to the Apostles' instruction and the communal life, to the breaking of bread and the prayers . . . They went to the Temple area together every day, while in their homes they broke bread . . . praising God" (Acts 1:14). And again: "They devoted themselves to constant prayer . . . with Mary, the Mother of Jesus" (Acts 1:14).

---

From *L'Osservatore Romano* No.47 (810) 21 November 1983
Title: "At Prayer with Mary, the Mother of Jesus"

In the community of believers at prayer, Mary is present, not only at the beginnings of the faith but in every time.

"She appears as such in the visit to the mother of the Precursor, when she pours out her soul in expressions glorifying God, and expressions of humility, faith and hope. This prayer is the Magnificat, Mary's prayer 'par excellence,' the song of the messianic times in which there mingles the joy of the ancient and the new Israel" (Paul VI's Apostolic Exhortation, *Marialis Cultus,* n.18). Mary appears as the Virgin in prayer at Cana, the Virgin in prayer in the Upper Room. "We have here the prayerful presence of Mary in the early Church and in the Church throughout all ages, for, having been assumed into heaven, she has not abandoned her mission of intercession and salvation. The title Virgin in prayer also fits the Church, which day by day presents to the Father the needs of her children, 'praises the Lord unceasingly and intercedes for the salvation of the world' " (ibid. 18).

* * *

1. In most of the Pope's messages, his first focus is on the People of God, the Church, and then he draws our attention to Mary and her place in this scheme.

2. We have been redeemed by Christ, our sins are forgiven and we share in his resurrection. These are the gifts of the Lord to us. In return we thank and praise the Lord our God, that is, we are a People at prayer.

3. From the earliest times the Church has been a Church at prayer. We pray in our assemblies, but also in our homes and in our daily lives. We continually exercise this priestly office of prayer.

4. Pope John Paul II points out three important places in the Scriptures where we see Mary as the Virgin in prayer: at the Visitation, at Cana and in the Upper Room with the Apostles after the Ascension of the Lord.

5. Mary was Jewish and in all her prayers we are able to hear the echo of all the hopes and aspirations of ancient Israel.

6. Once again the Holy Father reminds us of how Mary is a "type" or model for the Church. As Mary prays and intercedes for us, so the Church also prays daily for us and presents our needs to the Lord.

*November 20, 1983*
*Feast of Christ the King*

# Mary Anticipates Christ's Final Victory

The eschatological kingdom of Christ and of God (cf. Col 1:13) will be fulfilled when the Lord is all in everything, after destroying the dominion of Satan, of sin and of death.

The Kingdom of God is, however, already present in history "in mystery," and is at work in those who accept it. It is present in the reality of the Church, which is the sacrament of salvation and at the same time the mystery whose limits are known only to the mercy of the Father, who wills that all be saved. The sanctity of the Church here below prefigures the future fullness of the Kingdom.

The splendid expressions of the Letter to the Colossians with regard to the Kingdom (Col 1:13) apply to Mary, totally preserved from the oppression of evil: "He rescued us from the power of darkness and brought us into the kingdom of his beloved Son." It is in Christ that the Kingdom of God has made its entry into history, and those who have accepted it have become sharers in it: "Any who did accept him he empowered to become children of God. These are they who believe in his name" (Jn 1:13). Mary, the Mother of Christ and the faithful disciple of the Word, has entered into the fullness of the Kingdom. Her whole existence as a creature

---

From *L'Osservatore Romano* No.48 (811) 28 November 1983
Title: "Mary Is the Anticipation of Christ's Eschatological Kingdom"

loved by the Lord *(kecharitomene)* and enlivened by the Spirit is a concrete testimony and prelude of eschatological realities.

The Virgin Mary, already a sign and anticipation of future goods in her earthly life, now glorified beside Christ the Lord, is the image and the fulfillment of the Kingdom of God. She is the first to have followed Christ the "firstborn of many brothers," and the "beginning of the new creation" and "head of the Church" (cf. Col 1:18–20). She is the first to have inherited his glory. The glorification of Mary, our sister, is the most splendid confirmation of the words of Scripture: "Both with and in Christ Jesus he raised us up and give us a place in the heavens" (Eph 2:6). Her entrance into the eschatological Kingdom of God is the pledge and the guarantee of the participation of the whole Church, the Body of Christ in the glory of her Lord.

Tomorrow, the liturgical commemoration of the Presentation of Mary Most Holy, the Church celebrates the "Day of Cloistered Sisters," which recall the cloistered religious throughout the world. They, as the Second Vatican Council states, are members of those communities which are totally dedicated to contemplation, and give themselves to God alone in solitude and silence and through constant prayer and ready penance, and they occupy an eminent place in the Mystical Body of Christ. "For they offer God a choice sacrifice of praise. They brighten God's people by the richest splendors of sanctity. By their example they motivate his people; by imparting a hidden, apostolic fruitfulness, they make this people grow. Thus they are the glory of the Church and an overflowing fountain of heavenly graces" (cf. *Perfectae Caritatis,* 7).

The cloistered sisters—to whom I address today my good wishes and yours—are praying for us! It is therefore right that all the members of the Church respond to their intense and spiritual generosity with deep gratitude manifested in fervent prayer, in sincere esteem, and in concrete help for the needs, including economic ones, of these sisters of ours who have exemplarily and joyously vowed their lives to the Lord.

* * *

1. The word "eschatological" means the study of the final times. While we generally think of the "final times" as some thing future when we will be in heaven, the Holy Father points out that even now, today, we share in the mystery of Christ's victory over sin and death. When we are holy, we foreshadow the holiness of heaven.

2. Today the Holy Father reminds us of a different image or figure for the Church. The Church is the sacrament of salvation. The visible sign given to us by Christ to make us holy.

3. Quoting the Letter to the Colossians the Holy Father applies the words to Mary. This choice gives us a new insight into Mary's place in the scheme of salvation.

4. The Pope's message gives even more emphasis to the position of Mary. She already enjoys the fullness of Christ's victory. She has already been redeemed and is the first to be part of the Kingdom. As one "loved by the Lord" she is the prelude to the Kingdom. To clarify his meaning, he uses a Greek word *kecharitomene*—one loved by the Lord.

5. In Mary, our sister, we have our hope. What the Lord has done for Mary, the Lord has promised to do for us as well. She is the pledge and guarantee of the participation of all the faithful in the Kingdom, the eschatological Kingdom.

6. Almost every Sunday before or after the principle messages, the Holy Father will draw our attention to some important event or celebration which is worthy of consideration. Today the Holy Father reminded his audience of the consecration of the cloistered nuns and their important place in the Church.

*November 27, 1983*

# Advent: A Time of Special Devotion to Mary

Today, the First Sunday of Advent, we repeated the antiphon of the Responsorial Psalm: "I rejoiced when I heard them say, 'Let us go to the house of the Lord.' " We wish to add: "With Mary, let us go rejoicing to the house of the Lord." As the liturgists exhort us, and as Paul VI teaches, Advent is "a time particularly suited to devotion to the Mother of the Lord" (Apostolic Exhortation *Marialis Cultus,* 4) and to a suitable catechesis. This is an orientation that I hope will be "accepted and followed everywhere" (ibid.).

Joy is a fundamental element of the sacred season that begins today. Advent is a time of vigilance, prayer and conversion, in addition to being a season of fervent and joyful expectations. The reason is clear: the Lord is near (Phil 4:5), the Lord is with you or in your midst, as was announced to Mary (Lk 1:28) and to the daughter of Sion (Zep 3:15).

The first word addressed to Mary in the New Testament is a joyful invitation: exult, rejoice! This greeting is linked to the coming of the Savior. To Mary first is announced a joy that later will be proclaimed to all the people. She shares in this joy in an extraordinary manner and degree.

In her, the joy of ancient Israel is concentrated and

From *L'Osservatore Romano* No. 49 (812) 5 December 1983
Title: "Rejoice, O Highly Favored Daughter!"

reaches its fullness, and the happiness of messianic times bursts forth unrestrainedly. The Virgin's joy is particularly the joy of the "remnant" of Israel, the poor who await God's salvation and experience his fidelity. To share in this feast it is necessary to await the Savior with humility and to welcome him with confidence. "The faithful, living in the liturgy the spirit of Advent, by thinking about the inexpressible love with which the Virgin Mother awaited her Son, are invited to take her as a model and to prepare themselves to meet the saviour who is to come. They must be 'vigilant in prayer and joyful in praise' " (*Marialis Cultus,* 4).

* * *

1. Today the Holy Father builds his message as a reflection on St. Luke's Gospel and Psalm 122. "Joy" marks the Annunciation, this Psalm and the whole season of Advent.

2. Our devotions and our piety, the Holy Father reminds us, must reflect the Church and its liturgy. Thus, Advent is the real "month" of Our Lady.

3. "Joy" was the first word of the announcement of the redemption. "Rejoice, O highly favored daughter."

4. The joy of Advent is a special kind of joy. It is the joy of expectation. Not simply waiting, but waiting with expectation. The Lord is near.

5. One characteristic of the joy of Mary was that hers was the joy of all Israel. Because Mary is Jewish, she was able to experience this special joy of expectation of the coming Savior.

6. The Pope uses another image taken from the history of Israel, the image of the "remnant." They were the people who remained in Jerusalem during the time of the Exile. They were alone but they were faithful. They believed that the Lord was faithful as well. They joyfully and expectantly awaited the return of the Lord.

7. Finally the Holy Father invites us to model our joy on the joy of Mary as she awaited the birth of her Son. While we are vigilant in prayer and joyful in praise, we are asked to share that special joy of a mother awaiting the birth of her child.

*December 4, 1983*

# The World's Salvation is Linked to Mary's Faith

Salvation comes from heaven, but it also springs from the earth. The Messiah Savior is the Son of the Most High, but he is also the fruit of the womb of a woman, the Virgin Mary. The history of salvation, which is the history of a covenant with God, unfolds in a dialogue between him and his people. Everything is word and response. Mankind's response of faith must follow God's creative and salvific word. This logic is present to the greatest extent in the fundamental event of salvation, the Incarnation of the Son of God. Just as in Christ Jesus, the Word of the Father, all of God's saving acts are summed up, so in Mary's response the adherence of faith of God's people and all its members is summed up and reaches completion.

Mary, in particular, is the heiress and the completion of the faith of Abraham. Just as the patriarch is considered "our father" in the faith, so Mary, for all the more reason, must be claimed as "our mother" in the faith. Abraham is at the beginning, Mary at the summit of the generations of Israel. He anticipates and represents before God the people of the promise; she, a descendant of Abraham and a privileged heiress of his faith, receives the fruit of the promise. Through

From *L'Osservatore Romano* No. 50 (813) 12 December 1983
Title: "World's Salvation Linked to Mary's Faith"

Mary's faith and obedience, all the families of the earth are blessed, according to the promise made to Abraham (cf. Gen 12:3).

The Virgin's words, "I am the servant of the Lord. Let it be done to me as you say" (Lk 1:38), evoke not only the figure and attitude of Abraham, but the picture of all the servants of the Lord who have collaborated with him in the history of salvation. More generally, Mary's words recall the words of the children of Israel at the foot of Sinai on the day of the covenant: "We will do everything that the Lord has told us!" (Ex 24:3). Mary's response is personal, but it has also a community meaning. In her "yes" flows the faith of ancient Israel, and there is begun the faith of the Church. Her fidelity to the Lord, through a solidarity of grace, is a blessing for all who believe. The world's salvation is linked to her faith.

* * *

1. Earth and heaven, old and new, God and humankind, Word and response; the Pope speaks of many dialogues by which the history of salvation unfolds. Our response follows God's creative act. So it was with the most fundamental act of salvation, the Incarnation. Mary responded in faith to God's saving act.

2. Jesus Christ is THE saving act of God. Mary's response in faith is THE most important human response to God's initative.

3. Abraham is called our father in Faith in the First Eucharistic Prayer. So we may properly call Mary our mother in faith. Abraham initiated the response to God's call to us. Mary is at its summit. A promise is given to Abraham, the "fruit" was given to Mary.

4. By faith, Abraham was ready to offer his son in sacrifice. By faith Mary offered herself and later her Son to the Father.

5. Mary's words and example remind us of another event in the Hebrew Scriptures. At the foot of Mt. Sinai, when Moses told them of the covenant, the people responded: "We will do everything that the Lord has told us!" Mary's response was similar: "Let it be done unto me according to your word."

6. In a very profound insight the Pope reminds us that the "yes" of Mary flows from the faith of Israel and begins the faith of the Church. There is a "solidarity of grace" between her and the world's salvation.

*December 8, 1983*

# The Immaculate Conception

The feast of Mary's Immaculate Conception, which the Church joyfully celebrates today also as a significant moment in the Advent of the Savior, assumes in this Jubilee Year of Redemption a totally special theological and liturgical dimension. In fact, Mary's preservation from original sin from the first moment of her existence represents the first and radical effect of Christ's redemptive work, and links the Virgin, with a tight and indissoluble bond, to the Incarnation of the Son, who, before being born of her, redeems her in the most sublime way. This great Marian mystery, with which man's redemption begins in history, was already foreseen in that eternal plan of God the Father, in which Mary, preserved free from original sin in view of Christ's merits, was predestined to become in time the worthy mother of the same Savior. Besides being a sublime privilege that exalts Mary among all human creatures and the choirs of angels themselves, her sinless conception was the eminent condition of grace so that her whole person, from the very first instant, would be disposed in the most complete freedom, the freedom from original sin, to the service of Christ and his redemptive work, for all mankind.

---

From *L'Osservatore Romano* No. 50 (813) 12 December 1983
Title: "Mary's Immaculate Conception Brings Mankind to the Beginning of Creation"

Since the earliest centuries the Church has reflected on the "Fall from grace" and on the special way in which she was redeemed by Christ: through centuries of persevering research, with the celebration of the feast of her Conception becoming ever more widely spread, with the doctrinal interventions of its Magisterium, the Church with the venerated Pontiff Pius IX, in 1854 came to define as a truth of faith the doctrine that proclaims the Immaculate Conception of Mary.

In this truth that closely unites Mary to Christ, our faith very joyfully perceives a richness and variety of significance.

Seen in God's eternal plan for man, Mary is closely united to the Incarnate Word by an indissoluble bond of motherhood and is associated, from all eternity, to his redemptive work. For this mission of hers, it was fitting that there not be any stain of original sin in her from the first moment of her existence.

In the history of human generations, her Immaculate Conception represents the most perfect result of the gratuitous action of the Holy Spirit who forms her and makes her a new creation, virgin soil, a temple of the Spirit, from her very first moment. In this singular relationship lies the significant element of the faith that we are celebrating, since in Mary's conception, being born of man coincides with being reborn of the Spirit, and mankind is brought back to the beginning of creation.

Seen in the history and in the ways of the Redemption, Mary's Immaculate Conception signifies not only the first person to be redeemed, therefore the dawn of Redemption, but it also signifies that while for all the rest of the human race redemption means "liberation" from sin, for Mary, as much in need of redemption as all human beings, it means "preservation" from the same original sin, from the very first moment of her existence, in virtue of the merits of Christ, the one and only universal Redeemer.

* * *

1. The Immaculate Conception of Mary is of special significance in the Jubilee Year of the Redemption. Her Immaculate Conception reflects the close bond between her and her divine Son who redeemed her even before he was born of her! This is mystery!

2. Her Immaculate Conception was the first act in the unfolding of the eternal drama of redemption. It was a privilege for her, raising her above the angels and conferring on her complete freedom to be at the service of Christ and his redemptive work.

3. Mary was addressed by the Angel as "Full of grace." What did this form of address mean? Over the years the Church has studied these words, reflected on them, prayed about them publicly and finally declared that her Immaculate Conception is a truth of faith. The "magisterium" means the authentic teaching function of the Church.

4. The Holy Father offers a number of reflections on the significance of the Immaculate Conception:

a. It is a sign of the unity of Christ and Mary in the work of redemption and so it was fitting that she be without sin.

b. Her Immaculate Conception prepared her for the action of the spirit and brought us back to our original condition. For Mary being born coincided with being reborn.

c. Mary's redemption prevented her from being touched by sin. For us, redemption means freeing us from sin.

*December 11, 1983*

# Mary, the Image of the Church's Mystical Personality

On this Sunday of Advent that follows the feast of the Immaculate Conception and precedes, by just a short time now, the celebration of Christmas, and therefore the beginning of our redemption, our thoughts still linger on the rich significance of that great event of salvation that refers not only to the person of Mary, but also to the beginning of the new People of God, the Church of Christ, and the beginning of a new mankind that with her becomes the family of God. Mary, in fact, if she is considered in the fullness of the Church's mystery and its mission, expresses not only its autonomous personality, at the vertex and the the beginning of the Church, but in the dynamics of the history of salvation, she is also so intimately joined with the Church that she seems to be an embodiment and a living image of the mystical personality of the Church itself, the Spouse of Christ, signifying from the first moment of her existence all the wealth of grace that animates the Church. With regard to this, there comes to mind the precious information in the eighth chapter of *Lumen Gentium* which, interpreting St. Luke's perception, tells us: ". . . With her, the exalted Daughter of Sion, and after a long expectation of the promise, the

From *L'Osservatore Romano* No. 51 (814) 19 December 1983
Title:" Mary the Living Image of the Church's Mystical Personality"

times were at length fulfilled and the new dispensation established." That is, after the meeting between the Old and the New Covenant, Mary is the end of the messianic Church of Israel and the beginning of the newborn Church of Christ. It is she who is the ultimate and perfect expression of the ancient People of God, born of Abraham, and the first, sublime realization of the new People of children of God born of Christ. With Mary, therefore, the promises, the prefigurations, the prophecies and the spirituality of the Old Testament Church come to an end and there begins the New Testament Church, without stain or wrinkle, in the fullness of the grace of the Holy Spirit.

It is this ecclesiological dimension, proclaimed by the Second Vatican Council, that is the new itinerary that allows us to read and to understand in all its width and depth the mystery of Mary. Considered in this dimension, the Immaculate Conception of the Mother of God and our Mother acquires a richer ecclesial significance. With her, the masterpiece of God the Father and the purest reflection of the grace of the Holy Spirit, the Church of Christ begins. In Mary we see the immaculate conception of the Church, the temple and spouse without stain or wrinkle. It is in her that the Church feels it has attained its highest perfection, without a shadow of sin; and it is in her as the prototype, sign and help, that the ecclesial community, still a pilgrim on earth, is inspired and strengthened to advance in sanctity and in the struggle against sin.

* * *

1. If we look at the very last sentence of this message we are able to see more clearly what the Pope is saying. He calls Mary the "prototype" of the ecclesial community. "Prototype" means that what we can see in Mary we can also see in the Church.

2. Of course Mary is a person in her own right and the Lord has given her many graces and privileges. She is, after all, the first of

the believers and the Mother of the Redeemer. Mary, moreover, marks the beginning of a new People of God.

3. Repeating the same thought, the Pope sees Mary at the very center and beginning of the Church and united with the Church throughout its history. She is the living image of the mystical personality of the Church.

4. It is in Mary that the Old and New Covenants meet. She is the perfect expression of the children of Abraham and the sublime example of those born of Christ.

5. No longer do we deal with prophecies and types. Now in Mary we have the fullness of grace in the Holy Spirit.

6. Our devotion to Mary and our reflection on her privileges lead us to new insights into the mystery of the Church. In Mary's Immaculate Conception we see the Church in its highest perfection, without any shadow of sin.

7. While the Church is still on its pilgrim way, Mary is in heaven as its inspiration and strength.

4

# Mary, Blessed by the Lord

On this last Sunday of Advent, which directly prepares us for Christmas, what better inspiration could we find for our sentiments than to make our own what the very heart of the Virgin Mary experienced while awaiting the birth of the Lord? (cf. *Aperite Portas Redemptoris*, 6 January 1983,n.9).

In the expectation of this Virgin "blessed among women" (Lk 1:42), there is contained all the hope that the People of God had placed in the promises made by God to their patriarchs, and through the People of Israel, there is gathered the hope of all mankind.

We too try to make our own this awareness of Mary's faith, so deeply rooted in the history of her people and of all mankind, so as to grasp the essential meaning of its journey in the centuries and in the millenniums as a journey based on the hope of a salvation that comes from God.

Mary is happy because she believed that the Lord's words to her would be fulfilled (cf. Lk 1:45), knowing that God does not go back on his promises. She is "happy" and at the same time "blessed" by God. The two terms cannot be separated, and the first is the result of the second. Spoken by God, the word of blessing is always a source of life and therefore of happiness. For Scripture, happiness lies in generating and

---

From *L'Osservatore Romano* No. 51 (815) 18 December 1983
Title: "To Be Blessed Is to Be Happy"

communicating life, physical or spiritual. For this reason, whoever is "blessed" by God is "happy."

Mary's expectation is the expectation of generating life, but a life by which she herself is at the same time saved and made happy, because it is the Son of God himself.

Mary, before and more than any other believer, is the bearer of God's blessing, completed in Christ; and before and more than any other believer, she is blessed in Christ Jesus. Especially and uniquely suited to her are those words of the Letter to the Ephesians, where it is said that God "has bestowed on us in Christ every spiritual blessing in the heavens" (1:3).

By uniting ourselves to Mary's awaiting, we too will share in this divine blessing which, coming from the Father, is mediated to us by Jesus who is given to us by Mary.

* * *

1. People of faith can see what others cannot see. Thus St. Elizabeth could see Mary in a special way and could call her "blessed among women." All the hopes and all the promises of the People of Israel are found in Mary.

2. For us to grasp the central meaning of the mystery of the incarnation, we must go back to the Hebrew Scriptures, and like Mary, reflect on them with devout study to absorb the fundamental insights gathered over the centuries: "The Lord is coming."

3. In the Scriptures, happiness is blessedness and blessedness is happiness. We cannot separate the terms. We do not have one without the other. The person whom the Lord blesses is happy.

4. The Scriptures give us a special meaning for happiness. It is to be able to generate life, physical or spiritual. Thus Mary's happiness was special because the life she was generating physically was spiritual life as well.

5. God has given us every spiritual blessing in Christ. St. Paul says this of every Christian, but it is especially true of Mary.

6. If we unite ourselves to Mary in her special kind of waiting, we will also share with her a special blessing, a special happiness.

# Epiphany, A Significant Day for Our Salvation

On this Sunday, to which many countries have transferred the Epiphany of Our Lord, while celebrating the brilliant manifestations of the Savior to the people and the universal vocation to salvation, the Church contemplates also the Virgin Mother, who offers her Son to the adoration of the Magi. In fact, since ancient times, the Epiphany has been considered a significant moment in the Savior's incarnation and so also of Mary's divine motherhood. But, in the event narrated for us by St. Matthew (Mt 2:11), when she presents her Son to the Magi, Mary not only performs a personal act as mother, but she is also a figure of the Church which, as the mother of all peoples, in the person of Mary initiates its work of evangelization. This personal and ecclesial significance of the virginal motherhood of Mary in today's solemnity urges us to pause once more on the Virgin Mother to deepen our knowledge of the ecclesial value of this mystery.

In fact, Mary is the prototype of the Church in her virginal motherhood, an essential mystery which unites her to the Church in a common vocation and mission. Christ, as the Second Vatican Council states, was born of the Virgin Mary

---

From *L'Osservatore Romano* No. 3 (817) 9/10 January 1984
Title: "Significant Day for Our Salvation"

through the work of the Holy Spirit in order to be able to continue in a certain sense to be born and to grow in the Church, always through the work of the Holy Spirit.

Both Mary and the Church are living temples, sanctuaries and instruments through which and in which the Holy Spirit is manifested. In a virginal way, they give birth to the same Savior: Mary bears life in her womb and gives birth virginally; the Church gives life in the baptismal water and in the proclamation of the faith, giving it birth in the hearts of the faithful.

In the mystery of the Church, which in turn is rightly called Mother-Virgin, the Blessed Virgin Mary, first and in an eminent way, gives the example of the virgin and of the mother. In this close typological relationship, Mary's motherhood receives light and significance from the motherhood of the Church, of which she is a member and figure, and the Church's motherhood receives light and begins truly from Mary's motherhood, in which it already feels completely and perfectly realized. Like Mary, the Church too is a virgin and in giving birth to the children of God, wholly preserves faith, hope and charity.

The virginal motherhood which Mary and the Church have in common makes of them an indivisible and indissoluble unit, as in a sole sacrament of salvation for all men.

Let us rejoice, then, brothers and sisters, on such a significant day for our salvation in which the Savior, his Church and Mary appear to us intimately.

* * *

1. When we use the word "model" we understand that we want to imitate what we see in our model Mary. In this message the Holy Father says that Mary is more than a model, she is a "prototype" and "figure" for the Church.

2. Prototype and figure have a deeper meaning than just model. "Prototype" means the first of its kind. "Figure" means the plan

by which a second copy is made. The place of Mary in the Gospel of the Epiphany leads us to see Mary as both prototype and figure of the Church.

3. It was Mary who presented Jesus to the wise men, the Magi. They were gentiles, not Jewish so that Mary is the first to being the good news to the gentiles. She is the first evangelizer.

4. The Church is the favorite subject of Pope John Paul II. In today's complex Angelus message, he teaches us a new way to look at the Church. We must view the Church as we view the blessed Virgin.

5. Mary is virgin and mother. She conceived and delivered the Lord Jesus by the work of the Holy Spirit. The Church also by the work of the Holy Spirit gives birth to Jesus in the hearts of the faithful in the waters of baptism and in the preaching of the Word.

6. The term "virgin-mother" applied to the Church goes back to the second century. As the Holy Father uses the term, he reminds us that Mary is a member of the Church and as she gave birth to Jesus, so the Church gives birth to the faithful.

7. The relationship of Mary and the Church is so close and so intimate that the Holy Father uses a special term to describe it. Their union is a single "sacrament of salvation."

*January 15, 1984*

# Mary, the Generous Collaborator of Christ

"I will make you a light to the nations, that my salvation may reach to the ends of the earth" (Is 49:6).

These words from the second poem about the Servant of Yahweh are fulfilled in Jesus, servant of the Father, proclaimed by Simeon a light to the Gentiles and the glory of the people Israel (cf. Lk 2:32).

Both the Servant in the Book of Isaiah and Jesus—as is known—bring light and salvation through sacrifice.

This is what the Responsorial Psalm of today's Liturgy clearly emphasizes:

> "Sacrifice and oblation you wished not, but ears open to obedience you gave me. Holocausts or sin offerings you sought not; then said I, 'Behold I come' " (Ps 39(40):7–8).

Not only the Servant, not only Jesus, is called to carry out the will of the Father, to offer his life for the world's salvation: all the People of God, the Church, must do likewise.

---

From *L'Osservatore Romano* No. 4 (818) 23 January 1984
Title: "Pope Reminds Faithful of the Importance of Prayer for Unity of Christians"

For this reason we have repeated in unison: "Here am I, Lord, I come to do your will!"

Associated with Christ the Savior and his sacrifice, we contemplate above all the Virgin Mary, to whom Simeon, enlightened by the Holy Spirit, addressed the mysterious, prophetic words: "And you yourself shall be pierced with a sword" (Lk 2:35).

It is a pronouncement that will be fulfilled for Mary in the passion and death of her Son. Beside him who is wounded by the spear, there is on Calvary his Mother, whose soul is pierced by a sword. And the Word of God is compared to a sword (cf. Heb 4:12). Because of the Word which creates and destroys, which gives death and life; because the Word which Mary cannot always understand immediately, but which she welcomes and ponders and compares in her heart; because of Christ, the Word of the Father, contradicted by men, her soul is pierced by sorrow, as if by a sword. The Word, welcomed and lived in total obedience to the Father, makes the Virgin the generous collaborator of Christ the Savior. United with that of Christ, her sacrifice brings light and salvation to the Gentiles.

Every believer is called to offer his life together with Christ for the redemption of the world. Like Mary, all of us must "fill up" in our flesh "what is lacking in the sufferings of Christ for the sake of his body, the Church" (Col 1:24).

I want to call your attention today to a spiritual event of particular importance. Next Wednesday, January 18, the annual Week of Prayer for Christian Unity will begin. Throughout the entire world, Christians of various denominations will pray for the restoration of full unity. It is the Cross of the Lord which calls to unity. In fact, Jesus Christ died "to gather into one all the dispersed children of God" (Jn 11:52): yesterday, today and forever.

I warmly invite all Catholics to intensify their prayers during this week and to unite them to those of all the other baptized people, that our common Lord may grant that we praise him with one voice and heart.

* * *

1. For Pope John Paul II as for the Second Vatican Council, almost every consideration of Mary is in the context of the Church and the liturgy. This day the Scriptures pictured Jesus, Mary and Joseph at the presentation of Jesus in the Temple (Lk 2:22). The words of Simeon reflect the words of Isaiah and are fulfilled in Christ.

2. It is not Jesus alone but all of us, all the People of God who must be a light to the nations. All are to do the will of the Father.

3. Simeon also prophesied about Mary. She will be pierced by a sword. It is the Scriptures themselves, the Word of the Lord, which are this sword. That Word gives life and death: that Word which is too profound to comprehend: that Word which is the occasion for contemplation: that Word will pierce her heart.

4. Mary welcomed that Word with her generous "fiat." Her "yes" made her a generous collaborator with Christ in his sacrifice. United with Christ, she brings salvation to the nations.

5. The Pope reminds us that we too are called to live a life of sacrifice with Christ. Like Christ, and like Mary, we too must fill up what is lacking in their sufferings for the Body which is the Church.

6. As on other occasions, the Holy Father invites the prayers of the faithful for some important purpose. This time it is to ask all Catholics to pray fervently that all Christians may praise our one Lord with one voice and one heart.

*January 22, 1984*

# Mary the Believer

During the Advent season and the celebrations of Christmas we contemplated at length, beside Christ, the Virgin Mary. We approached the mystery of Christmas and we found the Child with Mary, "the Child and his Mother" (Mt 2:11,13).

In adoring the Son, we have venerated his Mother, proclaiming her blessed primarily and above all for her faith (cf. Lk 1:45;11:28).

Faith is never easy, and it certainly was not so for Mary. This is evidenced by the repeated praises addressed to her because of her faith: these praises highlight the value, the esteem, and certainly the difficulty of her believing. The words of the evangelist stress this explicitly: "But they did not grasp what he said to them" (Lk 2:50). Luke is not afraid to note the difficulty and even the lack of understanding, on the part of Mary and Joseph, of the words and the mystery of their Son.

The "incomprehension" of Mary, of Joseph, and of the disciples in general is evidently much different from the disbelief of those who have no faith in Jesus. We are dealing here with the difficulty of penetrating to the bottom, and immediately, the unfathomable depths of the person and the mystery of Christ. But it is a momentary "incomprehension"

---

From *L'Osservatore Romano* No. 5 (819) 30 January 1984
Title: "Mary's Faith Was Certainly Not Easy"

that leads to reflection, to meditation, to a wise attitude, so typical of Jesus' Mother, who kept and compared words and events in her heart (cf. Lk2:19,51).

Faith is indeed a light, but it is not the exhaustive understanding of the mystery. On the contrary, it is a reliance on God and his word that transcends the limits of human reason. It is a leaning upon him, seeking and finding in this attitude one's firmness and confidence. This is Mary's interior disposition, expressed once for all in the Annunciation: "I am the servant of the Lord. Let it be done to me as you say." A great faith, Mary's, a faith lived out and blessed: it is the faith of those who though they have not seen have yet believed (cf. Jn 20:29).

Mary's life, like ours, progresses day by day in faith and vision. The Council Observes: "Thus the Blessed Virgin advanced in her pilgrimage of faith, and loyally persevered in her union with her Son unto the Cross" (*Lumen Gentium,* 58). May she, the believer, accompany us along God's mysterious paths!

* * *

1. In the last line of this Angelus message, the Pope gives Mary a new title for us to use: "Mary the believer." Of course we have always known that Mary is a believer, but to call her by this new title is to give us a very helpful new insight into who and what Mary is.

2. Mary is never far from Jesus. We saw this in the Advent and Christmas celebrations. But as close as she is to Jesus, she did not understand completely who he was or what he was about. It is precisely in this situation that the Holy Father wishes to make his point. Mary is blessed because she believed, not because she knew.

3. "Incomprehension" is not the same as disbelief. Disbelief leads to the rejection of Jesus. Mary, rather, turns to reflection, meditation, contemplation and so to faith.

4. Even with the light of faith, we do not "know" everything. Rather, as with Mary, faith helps us go beyond human reason and find courage and strength to persevere in spite of difficulty.

5. When Jesus appeared to the Apostles after the resurrection, he told St. Thomas that many would be more blessed when, though they had not seen, they believed. It was the same with Mary. At the Annunciation she said "How can this be?" She did not see, yet she answered "Let it be done unto me."

6. In many of his messages, the Holy Father has called Mary the type and figure of the Church (see message of January 8, 1984). Here he points her out to us as our personal model, as one whom we must imitate.

*January 29, 1984*

# Mary in the Mystery of Cana

Today's Liturgy celebrates the dignity of the "poor in spirit," those who, like Christ, are meek and humble of heart. They are the holy remnant of Israel, the heirs of the promises, the bearers of the hope of the People of God. They will obtain the messianic blessings for themselves and for everyone. Mary is certainly one of them. "She stands out among the poor and humble of the Lord, who confidently await and receive salvation from him. With her, the exalted Daughter of Sion, and after a long expectation of the promise, the times were at length fulfilled and the new dispensation established" (*Lumen Gentium,* 55).

Mary has not only welcomed and given to the world its Savior, but she put her life entirely at the service of the Mystery of salvation. This work of hers appears especially evident in the mystery of Cana. This episode, in which appears the first of the "signs," that is, the miracles, of Jesus, offers a deeply theological and symbolic content.

Cana does not indicate merely (with the change of water into wine) the passing from the Old to the New Covenant, but it offers "in a retrospect sense" a summary of the Mosaic Covenant and "in a prospective sense" an anticipation of Jesus' "hour," that is, his glorification through the Cross.

---

From *L'Osservatore Romano* No. 6 (820) 6 February 1984
Title: "Mary in the Mystery of Cana"

In this eminently salvific context, the person and the work of Mary assume an exceptional importance. In her words, "Do whatever he tells you" (Jn 2:5), there is the echo of the words of the people of Israel at the time of the Covenant (Ex 19:8; 24:3,7; Deut 5:27), and Mary is the personification and sublime representative of that people.

The Mother of God not only expresses and carries to completion the attitude of the people of the Old Covenant, but her intervention at Cana also stirs up the faith of the disciples. Mary's faith is at the origin of the sign performed by Jesus and it prepares the disciples to accept the manifestation of his glory and to believe in him. She therefore assumes a guiding role in the birth of the faith community which begins to be formed around Jesus.

Mary's life is thus clearly oriented to the service of the Son of God and his mission. She is now the "Woman" by antonomasia: hers is a vocation that will reach its fullness when at the foot of the Cross she will become the "Woman-Mother" of the disciple and, through him, of the new people arising from Christ's sacrifice.

* * *

1. The Holy Father refers to the first reading of the day from the Book of Isaiah (62:1–5). The Prophet encourages those who have been waiting so long for their restoration. At the time of the Annunciation, this waiting was transferred to a hope for the Messiah.

2. The most surprising thing about this message is that it does not mention the "marriage" which took place. Rather, the Holy Father leads us into the deeper mystery of faith found here and to Mary's place in the unfolding of our salvation.

3. At Cana we are to look back (retrospective) into Jewish history and to look forward (prospective) to the Cross. After the Lord God (Yahweh) had given the commandments on Mt. Sinai, all the people said "What ever the Lord tells us, we will do." These words are echoed by Mary at Cana. Her words at Cana are just as true today.

4. The last words of the episode at Cana tell us that this is when the disciples began to believe in Jesus. Mary was there at the beginning of faith. It was her own faith in Jesus which helped prepare for their faith.

6. *Antonomasia* is a figure of speech in which the qualities of a name are used for the name itself. So while St. John in his Gospel never uses Mary's name, he uses "Mother of Jesus" and "his mother." On Calvary she is "woman." Her vocation, the Pope tells us is to be "Woman-Mother."

*February 5, 1984*

# Marian Piety Is Born of the Bible and the Altar

On this Sunday and, Lord willing, on the following Sundays, I will dwell with you on some aspects of Marian piety, that is, on the devout and filial love with which the disciples of Christ, in the East and in the West, venerate Mary Most Holy. This piety is the result of an exalting "Christian experience" in the sense that it is rooted in the mystery of Christ and finds in this mystery its origin and its justification, the reason for its development and the ultimate goal for which it reaches with an intimate dynamism.

"In the beginning was the Word, and the Word was in God's presence, and the Word was God," John writes in the prologue of his Gospel (Jn 1:1). And he adds, "Through him all things came into being" (Ibid.,3). All things. Even Mary. Or rather, above all Mary, who after Christ's sacred humanity constitutes the summit of creation, the "glory of the universe," as the Liturgy hails her (*Liturgy of the Hours,* 8 Dec., Hymn at Morning Prayer).

"All were created . . . for him" (Col 1:16), Paul the Apostle specifies. All. Including Mary. For him she was created: that she might be his holy Mother, and that the Word might

From *L'Osservatore Romano* No. 7 (821), 13 February 1984
Title: "Marian Piety Born of the Bible and the Altar"

be clothed with human nature in her virginal womb; that she might be his faithful disciple who in the treasure chest of a pure heart might preserve the word of life (cf. Lk 2:19,51); the new woman, placed beside him the new Man, the Redeemer of all men; that she might be the Ark of an unbroken Covenant: the image of the new People of God and of the new Jerusalem; the first and already mature fruit of the redemption.

"Through him . . . for him," the Scriptures tell us. Therefore everything in Mary relates to Christ, everything depends on him, everything is pervaded by his mystery.

Right from apostolic times Christians, contemplating Jesus "the Lord of glory" (cf. 1 Cor 2:8), and investigating the mystery of his person—Son of God and, through Mary, Son of man—have understood Mary's essential role in the work of salvation. Then, little by little, reflecting on Mary's indissoluble association in the saving events of the life, death and resurrection of Jesus, they have assumed in her regard an attitude of affectionate wonder, trusting homage, loving veneration.

As we know, the "mystery of Christ," in which Marian piety is rooted, through the action of the Holy Spirit has been translated into words and consigned to divine Scripture as an announcement of salvation and has been realized and celebrated in the sacred Liturgy as an event of grace.

In fact, when we examine ancient documentation and Sacred Tradition, we discover that Marian piety has its origin in meditation on the Bible and in the celebration of the divine mysteries. This happy observation, dear brothers and sisters, spontaneously turns into an anxious wish: that our piety toward the Mother of Jesus may remain always anchored in this twofold, genuine, ever fresh source: the Word of God and the Sacred Liturgy.

Let us entrust our prayer to the intercession of the Most Holy Virgin, Patroness of Lebanon.

* * *

1. What is the source of the deep and abiding love for Mary on the part of all Christians over the ages? The answer is Christ. The mystery of Christ is its origin, the reason for its development and its ultimate goal.

2. St. John's Gospel addresses the mystery of Christ "from the beginning" with the proclamation that through the Word, all things came to be. Mary came to be through Christ and after Christ, she is the crown and glory of the universe.

3. The Holy Father lists a number of ways in which Mary was created for Christ:

a. She was his mother,
b. He took his flesh in her womb,
c. She was his faithful disciple,
d. Her heart was a treasure chest to preserve the Word,
e. She was the the new woman standing beside the new Man,
f. She was the Ark of an unbroken Covenant.
g. She was the image of the new People of God and of the New Jerusalem.
h. She was the first and most mature fruit of the redemption.

4. Christians from the earliest times have recognized these truths about Mary and her central role in the redemption. They saw just how closely she was united to Christ Jesus in his birth, death and resurrection. It was only right, therefore, that they have venerated her and offered her homage and affection.

5. The truths of faith which the Scriptures have announced have been celebrated in the sacred liturgies. Any piety we have comes from a reflection on these Scriptures. Any love we may have for Mary will likewise be founded on the Word of God and the Sacred Liturgy.

6. On this Sunday the Pope chose to include in his Angelus address, an appeal for peace in Lebanon and for harmony based on real reconciliation among the various ethnic groups.

(Nota bene: In January 1985, the Rev. Lawrence Martin Jenco, O.S.M., confrere of the editor of this work was taken captive in Beruit, Lebanon and held hostage for eighteen months.)

*February 12, 1984*

# Mary is Present in Every Liturgical Action

Today I wish to dwell with you on the Blessed Virgin's presence in the celebration of the Liturgy.

As you know, every liturgical action, but above all the celebration of the Eucharist, is an occasion of communion and a source of unity.

Communion with God the Father, the Son and the Holy Spirit. In the sacred action, in fact, there comes to us the power of the Holy Spirit which, like a river of life, gushes from the eternal liturgy celebrated by the Risen Christ to the glory of the Father and for the salvation of man.

Communion of the heavenly Jerusalem with the Church still on pilgrimage along the paths of the world. In the celebration of the holy mysteries, heaven and earth are united, are illuminated by the same light, burn with the same charity, share in the same life, are blended in unity.

Communion among ourselves; in Liturgy we profess the same faith, share the same hope, are enlivened by the same love. Moved by the same Spirit, we invoke the same Father and, table companions of Christ, we are nourished by the same Word, the same Bread, the same Chalice of life.

But communion also and in a particular way with Mary,

---

From *L'Osservatore Romano* No. 8 (822) 20 February 1984
Title: "Mary Is Present in Every Liturgical Action"

the humble and glorious Mary. Why? Because the Liturgy is the action of Christ and of the Church.

The action of Christ. Because he is the only true "High Priest"(Heb 8:1): hidden under the veil of the sacred signs, he offers the sacrifice, baptizes, forgives sins, imposes his hands on the sick, announces the Good News, gives praise and glory to the Father, prays and intercedes for man (cf. *Sacrosanctum Concilium.* 7).

The action of the Church. Because "Christ indeed always associates the Church with himself in the truly great work of giving perfect praise to God and making men holy. The Church is his dearly beloved Bride who calls to her Lord, and through him offers worship to the Eternal Father" (ibid.).

Now the Blessed Virgin is intimately united to Christ and to the Church and she is inseparable from one and the other. She is therefore united to them in what constitutes the very essence of the Liturgy: the sacramental celebration of salvation to the glory of God and for the sanctification of man.

Mary is present in the memorial—the liturgical action—because she was present at the saving event.

She is at every baptismal font, where in faith and in the Holy Spirit the members of the Mystical Body are born to divine life, because with faith and with the power of the Holy Spirit she conceived its Head, Christ; she is at every altar, where the memorial of the Passion and resurrection is celebrated, because she was present, faithful with her whole being to the Father's plan, at the historic salvific occasion of Christ's death; she is in every upper room, where with the imposition of hands and holy annointing the Spirit is given to the faithful, because with Peter and the other Apostles, with the new-born Church, she was present at the inpouring of the Holy Spirit on Pentecost.

Christ, the High Priest; the Church, the community of worship; with both one and the other, Mary is incessantly united, in the saving event and in the liturgical memorial. In the life of every Christian as well, Mary must be present through a sincere and deep devotion.

* * *

1. As the Holy Father sets the foundation of our devotion to Mary, he gives us an instruction on the nature of the Church and the liturgy. He then goes on to show how Mary is present today in both since she was present to both as they were given to us by the Lord.

2. We are very familiar with the words "Holy Communion." Today the Angelus message takes some time to reflect on these words and the reality they represent. Communion means "in union with" or better still, "one with." We are one with the Father, Son and Spirit as eternal thanks is offered for the gift of salvation.

3. We who are still on pilgrimage are one with the heavenly Jerusalem in the celebration of the holy mysteries. We have the same light, share the same Word and receive the same Body and Blood.

4. In the liturgy, we remember what the Lord has done and, as we remember we make him present once again. As we remember Christ in his words and in his deeds we make him present among us once again in a sacramental way, in preaching, in forgiving and in announcing the Good News.

5. As we share in the action of the Church, that is, as we participate in the public worship, the liturgy, we are likewise united to Christ. With him we offer worship to the Eternal Father.

6. Mary is united with, "one with" Christ and the Church in a way which is more intimate than for any other creature. So she is one with Christ and the Church in each and every one of their actions.

7. Because of her union, her communion, with Christ, Mary is present at every Baptism for in her Christ was born. She is present at every Eucharist because she was present at Calvary. She is present at every gathering of the faithful when the Holy Spirit is poured out on them because she was present with the Apostles in the upper room.

8. Given all the ways she is present to us, we on our part must be present to her by our sincere and deep devotion.

*February 26, 1984*
*At Bari in Calabria*

+

# Mary, Queen of the Universe, Shows the Way to Unity

It has been a great joy for me this morning to crown the Icon of the "Odegitria" Virgin. I want in this way to pay homage to a very ancient Marian image that is much venerated also by our Orthodox brothers and sisters who have had, or have, the occasion to live or stay a while in this beautiful region of yours.

My act of veneration to the Most Holy Virgin through this famous and splendid Icon has therefore been intended also as a gesture extended to recognize and foster the ecumenical action which has been undertaken for centuries, and is still undertaken today, between Greeks and Latins in the light and under the protection of the Most Holy Mother of God.

The ceremony of crowning the image of the Virgin, as you know, is very old and traditional. Its symbolic significance is very clear: it is intended to express our acknowledgement of that spiritual and mystical "queenship" that Mary exercises, with Christ and under him, over the whole created universe, over heavenly creatures and earthly ones. We are speaking of that "queenship" whose various forms we celebrate and exalt when we recite the litanies and the Holy Rosary.

---

From *L'Osservatore Romano* No.10 (824) 5 March 1984
Title: "Mary, Queen of the Universe, Shows the Way to Unity"

Like her divine Son, Mary is not a "queen" of this world, but in the Kingdom of God, which, developing here below as an ecclesial reality, will come to completion in the heavenly Jerusalem. For this reason, the "kingdom" of Mary, like Christ's, is not one of those shortlived powers, not rarely based on injustice and oppression, but it is—as St. Paul says—a kingdom of "justice, peace and joy in the Holy Spirit" (Rm 14;17).

The "Odegitria" Virgin, as she points to her divine Son, shows us the the "way" to this kingdom, because it is precisely Jesus who is the Way. With this gesture, she shows us also the "way" to union among Christians, which consists in submitting, with absolute purity of intention and fervent consistency of life, to the spiritual royalty of Jesus and Mary.

May this day, so rich in ecumenical significance, be for everyone the occasion for a renewed commitment and a stronger hope in progress toward unity, with the intercession of the "Odegitria" Virgin, under the guidance of Christ and in the power of the Spirit.

* * *

1. *Odegitria* is Greek for "pointing the way." The icon or picture is one done in the Byzantine style much like the familiar picture "Our Lady of Perpetual Help" but of a different type of picture. In this icon, the Child Jesus is on the lap of Mary and she is pointing to him. "He is the way."

2. Icons have an immense importance in the devotional, spiritual and theological life of the Eastern Orthodox Church. The Pope, therefore, while on his pastoral visit to south eastern Italy in an area where there have been Greek Rite Christians for centuries, crowned this "Odegitria" Virgin. He sees it as an ecumenical act which may help bring about unity among Churches.

3. We call Mary "Queen" when we recite the Litanies of Mary and in one of the mysteries of the Rosary. We look upon her as a spiritual and mystical queen in the Kingdom of God which on earth is seen as relating to the Church.

4. The "kingdom" is special. It is a place of peace and joy. It is a place of justice.

5. Mary is Queen also because she shows us the way. She leads us by pointing out to us the "one way." That way is the Lord Jesus.

6. In addition to our personal devotion which is fostered by this Icon, the Holy Father reminds us that the way to Christian unity is the total submission to the spiritual royalty of Jesus and Mary.

For more information on this subject, see Michael O'Carrol's *Theotokos* published by Glazier, 1982 under "Icons."

*March 4, 1984*

# Mary's Love Accompanies Us to Heaven

At this Sunday's meeting I wish to continue the reflections on the Virgin's presence in liturgical celebration, the action of Christ and of the Church, to which Mary is indissolubly united. The Church has a deep conviction of this, which she derives from faith and, so to speak, from experience.

The Church indeed believes that the Blessed Virgin, assumed into heaven, is beside Christ, who forever lives to make intercession for us (cf.Heb7:25), and that the Mother's constant prayer is united to her Son's divine intercession: in heaven the Virgin's voice has become suppliant liturgy on behalf of men and women, her children, whom she contemplates in the light of God and whose needs and distress she knows.

The Church then has the intimate, vital, matured experience, in long centuries of the practice of prayer, of the active presence of the Virgin and of the angels and saints in the Liturgy. And she translates this experience, stored above all in liturgical prayer, into many attitudes of veneration, among which I wish to recall the need for the Virgin's motherly intercession and communion with her.

Within the framework of Christ's being the only Media-

---

From *L'Osservatore Romano* No. 11 (825) 12 March 1984
Title: "Mary's Love Accompanies Us to Heaven"

tor, God the Father has willed that the Virgin's maternal love accompany the Church on the path to our heavenly home. The Church therefore wants to travel that path with the Lord's Mother, whose voice excels in the praise of God, whose heart is full of anxiety in the pure oblation of itself and exults in the hymn of thanksgiving to the Most High.

On this day when we observe the Fifth Centenary of the death of St. Casimir, I wanted to be spiritually united with the bishops of Lithuania, who yesterday, at the tomb of the Saint of Vilnius, began the solemn jubilee celebrations in honor of their heavenly Patron.

A son of Casimir IV Jagellone, king of Poland and Grand Duke of Lithuania, St. Casimir in his short life of twenty-six years was distinguished for his adamant faith, his constant prayer, his crystal-clear purity, his active love for the poor and needy, his fervent devotions to the Most Holy Virgin. Because of his exemplary witness and various bonds of relationship, the Saint's life is linked to the civil and religious history of the Europe of his time.

The presence of representatives from the European Episcopal Conferences at today's celebration in Saint Peter's has therefore emphasized this common cultural and spiritual heritage that unites the various nations of Europe and furthermore recalls the "Christian roots" that have for centuries made fruitful and nourished all the manifestations of the history of this continent. Their presence has also expressed the affections, solicitude and solidarity of the Church of Europe toward all the People of God who are in Lithuania.

To all Lithuanians who are living in their homeland or who are dispersed throughout the world, I address my sincere wishes—accompanied by prayer to the Lord—that they may be always faithful to the precious spiritual heritage of their Patron Saint, firm in the faith of their ancestors, happy in hope, rooted in love and in communion with God, with the Church and with their brothers and sisters.

* * *

1. Without using the expression, the Holy Father here outline the idea of the "Communion of Saints." Mary has been assumed into heaven where she is united to Christ in a special way. In this union she continues to intercede for all her children. The Pope calls her intercession for us a liturgy.

2. The Church may properly be considered a community at prayer. Prayer is its constant occupation. Thus the Pope reminds us that this whole complex of prayer is best preserved in the liturgy. In turn, this expresses itself in veneration and especially in the need for Mary's intercession and our union with her.

3. United with Christ, the one Mediator, the Church unites its praise of God with Mary's praise for her praise excels all of ours. The Church identifies with Mary's heart which is so full. The Church knows that she still praises God as a pure oblation, a total giving of herself. Most of all, the Church unites with Mary in her exultant hymn of thanksgiving.

4. This Sunday the Holy Father seems to cut short his reflection on Mary to expand on a second theme, that of St. Casimir, patron of Lithuania.

*March 20, 1984*

# Mary Is Ever the Attentive and Caring Woman

On this first Sunday of Lent, which calls us to a renewed path of conversion, our glance turns to Mary, the perfect image of the Church. In her, in fact, we contemplate the creature with a new heart, the attentive and caring Woman, the disciple who could listen and pray without ceasing, the Virgin of the silent sacrifice.

Mary is the creature of the "new heart," proclaimed by the prophets. God had promised: "I will give you a new heart and place a new spirit within you" (Ez 36:26). Mary's historical experience, beginning with her Immaculate Conception, all unfolded under the shadow of the Spirit. But especially at the Annunciation she received from the Holy Spirit that "new heart" that made her docile to God, capable of accepting his plan of salvation and corresponding to it with absolute fidelity during her whole life. She is the "*Virgo fidelis,*" the faithful Virgin who epitomizes ancient Israel and prefigures the Church, espoused to God for ever in fidelity and love (cf. Hos 2:22).

Mary is still the attentive and caring Woman with regard to the spiritual and material needs of the brethren. The Gos-

---

From *L'Osservatore* Romano No. 12 (826) 20 March 1984
Title: Mary, Ever the Attentive and Caring Woman"

pel evidences her care toward the elderly Elizabeth; her discreet intervention at the marriage feast of Cana, to the joy of the young couple; the motherly acceptance of the disciple and of all the redeemed at the foot of the Cross. We are certain that from heaven she still carries on her mediation for the exiled children of Eve.

Mary is besides a disciple who embodied the Gospel right up to the sacrifice and martyrdom by the bloodless "sword" that Simeon had foretold in the Temple, uniting her lot to the bloody sacrifice of her Son. In the face of God's disconcerting offer, she never hesitated to repeat daily the "Yes" of the Annunciation, so that it became the "Yes" of the Easter for herself and for the whole human race.

* * *

1. What we see in Mary we are to reflect in our own lives for Mary is the perfect image of the Church. In Lent, the Holy Father reminds us, the call to conversion, the call to have a new heart within us, is exemplified by Mary.

2. The promise God had given to Israel to give them "a new heart" was accomplished in a special way in Mary. It began with her Immaculate Conception and was manifest especially in the Annunciation. There she showed her docility to God, accepting with generosity, his plan of salvation.

3. In the Prophet Hosea, the Scriptures use the image of a faithful husband, one who never wavers no matter what the provocation, to illustrate the love God has for his People. It is this kind of love which Mary has for the Lord. She is the faithful Virgin.

4. How does she reveal this "new heart?" Her visit to Elizabeth, her intervention at Cana and on Calvary show us her new heart. It is especially on Calvary that she received St. John and all the disciples as her beloved children.

5. The sword which Simeon had foretold at the Presentation in the Temple was the instrument which united her whole life to the Passion and Death of her Son. She never hesitated. The "Yes" of the Annunciation would become the "Yes" of Easter.

6. In the first paragraph of this message, the Holy Father spoke of Mary as the disciple who could listen and who could pray without ceasing. He does not develop these two attributes in this message but they also give us something to reflect on.

# Mary and Human Suffering

At the end of this celebration we prepare to recite the Angelus by reflecting on "Mary and human suffering."

"Rejoice, Jerusalem! Be glad for her, you who love her!" In this antiphon of the fourth Sunday of Lent, I like to see, through the words of Isaiah that the liturgy applies to the Church, the mystery of the Virgin Mother, the mystery of her joy and her maternal suffering. Because Mary is the true Daughter of Sion, the spiritual epitome of ancient Jerusalem, the beginning and summit of Christ's Church; moreover, she is the new Eve, the true Mother of all the living.

She, as the Daughter of Sion, and as the new Eve, is invited to rejoice today. Human suffering, in fact, cannot be understood except in the context of a lost happiness; and suffering makes no sense except in view of a promised happiness. "Rejoice, Jerusalem!"

Jerusalem's suffering, sung by the prophets, was the result of the infidelities of her children, which had brought about God's chastisement and exile from their homeland. The suffering of this mysterious new Daughter of Sion, Mary, is a result of the innumerable sins of all Adam's children, sins that have caused our expulsion from Paradise.

In Mary, therefore, in a unique way, there is revealed the

---

From *L'Osservatore Romano* No. 15 (829) 9 April 1984
Title: "Mary's Suffering Caused by the Sins of All Mankind"

salvific mystery of suffering, and the significance and fullness of human solidarity. Because the Virgin did not suffer for herself, being All Beautiful, the Ever Immaculate One: she suffered for us, in so far as she is the Mother of all. Just as Christ "bore our infirmities and endured our sufferings" (Is 55:4), so also Mary was weighted down as by the sufferings of childbirth through an immense motherhood that makes us reborn to God. The suffering of Mary, the new Eve, alongside the new Adam, Christ, was and still is the royal path to the reconciliation of the world. "Rejoice, Jerusalem! Exult with her, all you who were mourning over her!"

In the figure of the Virgin Mary, marked by suffering because of the infidelity of her children, but called to exult in joy in view of their redemption, our suffering finds its place: we too can become "a particle of the infinite treasures of the world's Redemption" (*Salvifice Doloris,* 27), that others might be able to share this treasure and attain to the fullness of joy that it has earned for us.

* * *

1. When the Prophet Isaiah exhorted Jerusalem to rejoice, he was telling them that through their present sufferings, a saviour would come. Joy would come from their sufferings. The liturgy applies this to the Church and now the Pope applies it to Mary. She is the Daughter of Sion, and through her sufferings, good will come forth.

2. The Prophet Isaiah indicated that the sufferings of Jerusalem were due to its infidelity, its sin. The sufferings of Mary, however, are not the result of any personal sin but rather because of the sins of all humankind. Sin had its beginning in the Garden of Eden.

3. The Pope speaks of the sufferings of Mary as the sufferings of childbirth. In her sufferings she was united to the new Adam and so becomes the new Eve, the new mother of the faithful. As a mother rejoices at the birth of her child, so Mary rejoices in the birth of the faithful.

4. The Holy Father had written an encyclical about human suffering which is called "Salvifice Doloris" (The Saving Value of

Suffering). He refers to this encyclical as he reminds us that as we reflect on the sufferings of Mary, we can see more clearly how we also participate in some small way in the infinite treasures of the Redemption.

*April 8, 1984*

# The Akathistos Hymn

The arrival of the noon hour invites us to address our thoughts to Mary with the Angelus prayer.

We are now very close to the days of the Lord's passion, and the Liturgy decisively directs us to Easter. But we cannot forget, especially during this Jubilee Year of the Redemption, the mystery from which everything has flowed and which remains the constitutive foundation of our reconciliation with God: the mystery of the Incarnation.

During these very days, in the Churches of the Byzantine Rite, a meaningful Marian liturgical celebration has taken place: the celebration of the Akathistos, a famous hymn that has been sung, standing, everywhere for many centuries in honor of the Mother of God. Monastaries and parishes, especially in our sister Orthodox Churches, have celebrated this liturgy with deep piety and intense participation, singing the praises of the Virgin in the heart of the mystery that saves: the mystery of the Incarnate Word and of his Church.

"Hail, through you joy rises; hail; through you sorrow fades."

So begins that ancient hymn, the object of a liturgical feast of its own. The presence of the Virgin in the economy of God, in fact, expands as the mystery of the humanity of Christ, the

---

From *L'Osservatore Romano* No. 16 (830) 16 April 1984
Title: "Union among Churches through Mary's Intercession"

living sacrament of the unity and salvation of the human race, expands. Wherever Christ irradiates his salvific action, there is mysteriously present his Mother, who clothed him in flesh and gave him to the world.

Mary is present at the mystery that one day was carried out in her womb, making her a throne of God that is more shining than a throne of the angels: "Hail, O most holy throne of him who is seated above the cherubim." She is present in the outpouring of peace and pardon that God lavishes on the world through her: "Hail, mercifulness of God toward man." She is present in the mercy that continues to be poured forth in abundance, in the grace that clothes us in light: "Hail, field that produces an abundance of mercies." She is present on the lips of the Apostles who proclaim the Word and in the witness of the martyrs, who go to their death for Christ: "Hail, unconquerable daring of the martyrs." She is present on the journey of faith that leads catechumens to Baptism, in the sacraments that give life and nourish the Church: "Hail, you are the fount of the holy martyrs, you are the spring of abundant water, you are the life of the Holy Banquet." She is present in the Church's pilgrimage toward the heavenly homeland through the desert of the world: "Hail, through you we lift our trophies: hail, through you conquered enemies fall." She is present beside each one of us who trusts in her: "Hail, medicine for my body, salvation of my soul!"

So sings this ancient hymn, composed when the Churches were still united. May it be a prelude to the times when all the Churches will find themselves reconciled and reunited, through the power of God and the intercession of the Virgin, in the one faith and in the one praise.

This we await, working and praying for it.

* * *

1. One of the directives which come to us from the Second Vatican Council is to have our prayer reflect the liturgical seasons.

This is the reason that the Pope explains why the Angelus is appropriate even though Holy Week and Easter are near. It is from the incarnation that all mysteries flow.

2. The meaning of the name of this Byzantine hymn, the *Akathistos* is simply "standing." There are two hymns with this same title, one in honor of Christ, the other in honor of Mary. They are sung "while standing," a special mark of respect. They are hymns, the Pope reminds us, which were composed when the Churches were one.

3. The more we know about Christ, about his work for our salvation, the more we can appreciate the part played by Mary. In whatever Christ does, Mary his mother is united with him. She gave him his flesh.

4. The Pope takes from the Akathistos Hymn various phrases which are directed to Mary and sees mirrored in them a reflection of ourselves. She is the throne, she is the source of mercy and abundant grace. She is our strength, she is our health.

5. The Holy Father desires that the use of this Hymn which had been composed when the Churches were one, may serve to implore the intercession of Mary that we may all be one. First we must be reconciled.

*April 15, 1984*

# Behold Your Mother

As the hour of the Angelus draws near, our thought, at the beginning of Holy Week, goes to Calvary, where the Mother of Jesus stood by the Cross (cf. Jn 19:25), and also a young man, John, the disciple whom Jesus loved (Jn 19:26), the disciple who at the Last Supper rested his head on the Lord's breast (cf. Jn 13:25), "drawing from his breast the secrets of wisdom and the mysteries of mercy" (Ambrose, *De institutione virginis,* 46). He wrote and consigned to the Church that which the other Evangelists did not say: "There stood by the Cross of Jesus his Mother."

The long silent itinerary of the Virgin, beginning with the joyous "Fiat" of Nazareth, clouded by obscure predictions at the offering of her First-born in the temple, found on Calvary its salvific coronation. "The Mother with piteous eye beheld the wounds of her Son, from which she knew would come the salvation of the world" (ibid. 49). Crucified with her crucified Son (cf. Gal 2:20), she contemplated with the anguish of a mother and with the heroic faith of a disciple the death of her God; "and lovingly consented to the immolation of this Victim which she herself had brought forth" (*Lumen Gentium,* 58) for that Sacrifice. Then she pro-

From *L'Osservatore Romano* No. 17 (831) 24 April 1984
Title: "Take the Blessed Virgin Mary into Your Hearts and Lives"

nounced her final "Fiat," doing the will of the Father on our behalf and gathering us all as her children, in accordance with Christ's testament: "Woman, behold your son!" (Jn 19:26).

"Behold your Mother!" said Jesus to the disciple; "and from that hour the disciple took her to his own home" (Jn 19:27). The virgin disciple took the Virgin Mother as his light, his treasure, his good, as the most precious gift inherited from the Lord. And he loved her tenderly with the heart of a son. "Therefore it does not surprise me—writes Ambrose—that he should have narrated the divine mysteries better than the others, he who had beside him, the dwelling place of the divine mysteries" (Ambrose, ibid., 50).

Young people, may you also take Mary into your hearts and into your lives: may she be the inspiration of your faith, the luminous star on your Paschal journey, to build a new world in the light of the Resurrection, while awaiting the eternal Easter of the Kingdom.

* * *

1. The silhouette of the Cross with Mary and John beside it, is among the most familiar Christian scenes. It is to this picture that the Pope draws us in this final Angelus message of this series. "There stood by the Cross of Jesus . . ."

2. What had begun with joy in Nazareth, was clouded by the predictions in the temple, now comes to its conclusion on Calvary. Now at last she knew the meaning of Nazareth as well as the meaning of those predictions. She was able to see with her own eyes the source of salvation.

3. The "fiat" given at Nazareth is given again on Calvary. This time the "fiat" results in all of us being given to her as her children. "Woman, behold your son!"

4. St. Ambrose suggested that because St. John was so close to Jesus and then so close to Mary, he was able to share the divine mysteries more deeply than the other apostles. Mary, he tells us, was the "dwelling place of the divine mysteries."

5. John saw Mary as a light, a treasure, a good and precious gift. Do we see that she is the same for us? He loved her with the heart of a son. Can we do less?

6. There were some 300,000 young people in St. Peter's Square this Palm Sunday. It was to them that the Holy Father addressed the last words of this message. Mary is our star and in the light of this star, we are to build a new world.

# More Marian Books and Tapes from the World Apostolate of Fatima

37362 *FATIMA IN LUCIA'S OWN WORDS*- This book of memoirs by Sr. Lucia is one of the outstanding works of Catholic Literature of our time. 200 pp., paper .......... $5.95

35529 *"THERE IS NOTHING MORE"*- The Rosary, scapular, Immaculate Heart and the Fatima Message. 368 pp., paper .......... $ 5.95

38195 *BEHOLD YOUR MOTHER:American Bishops' Pastoral Letter*- Concerns authentic Marian devotion. 66 pp., paper .......... $ 3.75

38229 *CITY OF GOD*- Detailed life of the Blessed Virgin by Mary of Ageda. 4 volumes, 2676 pp., hardcover .......... $49.00

38263 *CITY OF GOD (Abridged)*- Single volume abridgment of the *City of God.* 794 pp., paper .......... $12.50

38350 *A HEART FOR ALL*- The Immaculate Heart of Mary in the message of Fatima. 207 pp., hardcover .......... $ 3.95

38385 *MOTHER OF THE REDEEMER*- Encyclical letter of Pope John Paul II. Summarizes the Church's Marian teaching. 79 pp., paper .......... $ 1.50

38390 *SERMONS OF ST. FRANCIS DE SALES ON OUR LADY*- Teachings on Mary from a saint and doctor of the Church. 219 pp., paper .......... $ 8.00

38417 *THE GLORIES OF MARY*- by St. Alphonsus de Liguori. A glorious book about Mary. 670 pp., paper .......... $ 5.00

38518 *TRUE DEVOTION TO MARY*- by St. Louis Grignion de Montfort. A classical masterpiece on true devotion, showing the need to go to Jesus through Mary. 85 pp., paper .......... $ 4.50

38145 *FIRST LADY OF THE WORLD-A Popular History of Devotion to Mary*- by Peter Lappin. 192 pp., paper .......... $ 9.95

38133 *DICTIONARY OF MARY*- Sets forth the most important Catholic teachings about Mary in dictionary form. 416 pp., paper .......... $ 6.00

37447 *FATIMA: THE GREAT SIGN*- by Francis Johnston. The role of Fatima in the Church. 152 pp., paper .......... $ 4.95

37549 *MEET THE WITNESSES*- by John M. Haffert. Interviews with witnesses of the miracle of the sun. 160 pp., illustrated, paper .. $ 3.25

37583 *OUR LADY OF FATIMA*- by William T. Walsh. A classic account of the apparitions. 223 pp., paper .......... $ 4.95

49703 *"AND FROM THAT HOUR. . ."*- Pope John Paul II's historic homily at Fatima, May 13, 1982 .......... $ .50

49716 *THE SIGNIFICANCE OF MARY FOR WOMEN*- by Dr. Joyce A. Little .......... $ .50

**40983** *17 PAPAL DOCUMENTS ON THE ROSARY*- Contains Marialis Cultis. Superb reference. 150 pp., paper .................... **$ 2.00**

**51313** *BROWN SCAPULAR OF MOUNT CARMEL*- by Fr. Barry Bossa, S.A.C. Illustrated history, 50 pp., paper. .................... **$ 2.50**

**Audio Tapes**

**361564** *Mary In the Scriptures* by Msgr. James Turro ............... **$ 3.95**

**361569** *True Devotion to Mary* by Sr. Mary Frederick, M.C. .......... **$ 3.95**

**362147** *Fifteen decades of the Rosary* and Rosary history ............ **$10.95**

**361915** *The First National Fatima Symposium.* Study the message of Fatima in depth. Hear all the presentations in this six cassette album ................................................ **$24.00**

**362745** *Mother Teresa* speaks to pilgrims at the Blue Army Shrine of the Immaculate Heart of Mary. Fr. Frederick Miller addresses Total Consecration to Jesus through Mary (side 2) ................ **$ 4.95**

---

NAME ____________________

STREET ____________________

CITY ____________________

STATE ______________ ZIP ________

**World Apostolate of Fatima**
**(The Blue Army, USA)**
Mountain View Road
P.O. Box 976
Washington, NJ 07882
(201) 689-1700

| Qty. | Item # | Color/Description | Price Each | Total Price | |
|---|---|---|---|---|---|
| | | | | | |
| | | | | | |
| | | | | | |
| | | | Subtotal | | |
| | | | N.J. residents: Add 6% sales tax | | |
| | | | **Shipping & Handling** | | |
| | | | Donation | | |
| | | | Total* | | |

Please add proper shipping and handling charge shown below

| **Value of Order** | **USA** | **Foreign** |
|---|---|---|
| $0 - $1.99 | $.90 | $2.00 |
| $2.00-$24.99 | $3.00 | $5.00 |
| $25.00-$49.99 | $4.50 | $8.00 |
| $50.00-over | $6.50 | $12.00 |
| Over $100 | Add 10% | Add 15% |

Marian Reflections

Please make checks payable to: **World Apostolate of Fatima**

*** U.S. funds payable through a U.S. bank. Postal money orders in U.S. funds accepted.**

*Prices subject to change without notice*

P-93 ★
1~~6~~0~~4~~
108
17 ★
107 ★